Breaking New Ground

Community Development with Asian Communities

Jean Ellis

in association with
David Appleton, Peter Dale, Christopher Ensor,
Mohammed Habeebullah, John Hargreaves, Peter Hirst,
Meena Kumari, Sue Little, Hanif Malik and Mohammed Salam

Published in association with Community Projects Foundation

Bedford Square Press

Published by
Bedford Square Press of the
National Council for Voluntary Organisations
26 Bedford Square, London WC1B 3HU

First published 1989

British Library Cataloguing in Publication Data

Ellis, Jean
   Breaking New Ground: community
   development with Asian communities –
   (Community action).
   1. Great Britain. Community work with
   ethnic minorities
   I. Title II. Series
   302.8.4.00941

   ISBN 0–7199–1238–5

Typeset by The Wordshop
Printed in Great Britain by
Billing & Sons Ltd, Worcester

Contents

The opinions expressed in this book represent those of the author and those of the acknowledged individuals contributing to or collaborating in the publication. They do not necessarily represent the opinions, views or policy of the following agencies and authorities: Cleveland County Council, Manchester City Council, Rochdale and Metropolitan Borough Council, Community Projects Foundation, Al-Hilal Project and Rochdale Voluntary Action.

Foreword

One of the greatest assets of community development, as a method of working, is its ability to reach many of those people whose level of involvement rarely extends beyond the home or immediate family.

Often unseen, they are consequently unheard by those in authority. They have decisions made for them and things done to them, but seldom, if indeed ever, have the opportunity to participate in any decision-making process.

This book reflects the Community Projects Foundation's ongoing commitment to enabling local people to build better communities across the country. In particular those people who, for various reasons, find themselves excluded or marginalised from the wider community in which they live.

Working with Asian communities is an area of community development that until now has not been well documented. As this book demonstrates, it calls for the development of new skills and the adaptation of older methods to meet new needs.

Over the last 21 years CPF has gained practical experience in over fifty different projects, many, like Rochdale Community Project or the Islington Co-operative Development Agency, working directly with the local Asian community.

Breaking New Ground is the result, not only of CPF's experience, but that of a number of organisations working in the community development field with Asian communities in the northern towns and cities of Rochdale, Manchester and Middlesbrough. It is also a reflection of CPF's commitment to disseminate the lessons of good practice wherever they are found. It will, I hope, provide a useful and practical reference point for future community development projects.

David Thomas
Director, Community Projects Foundation

Introduction

This book represents a sharing of experience and an exercise in self-development by those who were involved. We hope that it will encourage more of the same: that is, training in its broadest interpretation. Much of existing training for community workers takes place 'on the job'. This is in part a reflection of the varied backgrounds of community workers and their desire not to mystify their occupation by closing it off to local activists who rarely come from academic backgrounds. While such training can thus draw lessons from immediate experience, it fails, like more formal academic training, to meet the demands of community work in multi-racial Britain.

When starting to work with Asian communities in the early 1980s, all the workers who contributed to this study experienced a real sense of isolation, and of breaking new ground. There was surprisingly little analysis to be found of the issues which were of concern, whether to individuals, or at a team level. It seemed necessary to attempt, not so much to find answers, but to analyse their experience in a way which might be of use to others, and more importantly, to break through the silence and stimulate a debate, raising the profile of the questions which were being raised.

We hope this book will talk directly not just to community workers and local activists but to their managers, supervisors and trainers, and to the policy makers, management committee members of community projects and non-statutory agencies, local government officers and politicians. What is only too clear in the text is that such people only too frequently turn to one or two individuals in the Asian community – 'key personalities', represented on numerous committees, but not necessarily representing the broad spectrum of the community. The challenge must be to reappraise and analyse the issues thoroughly rather than to respond to those individuals most acceptable politically, or whose demands can be most easily accommodated within existing policy initiatives.

Undoubtedly there are those who fail to see the need for increased levels of information. Where this is not the case, there is a real problem in the nature of the written material available to policy makers and managers. There is a body of material on community development which moves between the highly academic and theoretical on the one hand and detailed case study which fails to go forward to more general analysis on the other. In both cases it may be difficult for readers to draw parallels with their own immediate situation or neighbourhoods, and seldom is such writing drawn from work with black groups.

For those working with black groups the need has often been seen to be met by theoretical writing on anti-racism and racism awareness or broader anti-racism training. Racism awareness training started from the individual white person's own racism and the way this is drawn from and contributes to individual racism. Other forms of anti-racist training may aim to assist the individual worker to develop strategies to confront and challenge racism. But even when this training is done well it suffers inevitably from the limitations of a training which often takes place away from the working environment. What is urgently required is an attempt to reinterpret the theory and practice of community development in relation to day-to-day work in a multi-racial society.

In 1986, the need to discuss and share ideas provided the impetus which brought together community workers and community work managers from three towns in the north of England. The director of a community work project in Rochdale made use of links he had with workers in Middlesbrough and Manchester to draw together a group which quickly recognised themes and problems familiar to all three areas. Community work with Asian communities, in common with many aspects of community work with white communities, raises many difficult and complex issues. Both the methods of work and the outcome may threaten the established order, whether in the neighbourhood or beyond, and such work frequently has a high political profile. However, the existence of racism, both within employing agencies and within communities, served to compound the problems associated with the management of such work.

As members of the group began to pick their way through these issues, they decided to put in writing the problems and solutions, the good practice as well as the mistakes, so that others might benefit from their experience. This emerging objective coincided with the Community Projects Foundation's aim of extracting and disseminating learning from fieldwork practice. It was with CPF's resources and assistance, then, that a freelance writer was employed to research, describe and analyse the material. There were advantages in using someone who would be sufficiently separate from the events to bring to the job a fresh level of critical analysis, while at the same time attempting to reflect and describe the differing approaches of all the workers concerned.

The book was never intended to be a comprehensive analysis of community development with black communities. It was always an attempt by a group of individuals and their agencies to evaluate their own practice, organisation and management. There will inevitably be gaps, areas of work which will not be described, different approaches and different contextual frameworks. It seemed valid to focus specifically on work with Asian communities. Given the population characteristics of the areas in which the agencies were working, these were by and large the groups with which the workers had contact. Yet it will be apparent that many of the principles emerging from the discussion are relevant not only to work with Asian groups but to work with black communities more generally.

Neither was it ever the intention of the group nor that of the writer to focus on the black communities themselves. Criticism has understandably frequently been made of discussion of work with black communities that by implication, if not explicitly, it places the problem with the community itself. Our belief was that, while an understanding of community characteristics should at times be made explicit, it was institutional assumptions and responses that were inappropriate and inadequate, and that this was where attention needed to be directed. Therefore, while some members of community projects were interviewed, those contributing to the book have been in the main workers in agencies, their managers, council politicians and officers. The study looks at issues specific to the communities themselves as they highlight inappropriate structures, ways of working and management. Many of the issues are applicable not only to agencies which work with black communities; there are many points made in the text which challenge the structure and function of any agency.

The detailed experience from which analysis was drawn remained limited to three towns in northern Britain, each of which had its own specific socio-economic and political characteristics. Workers in these three towns, although aware of the high profile of race-related issues in the south of England, had not faced similar community or political awareness within their own localities, with the exception of parts of Manchester. For this reason the approach emanating from some London boroughs, for example, did not always seem immediately transferable. The group possibly experienced a freedom to describe and analyse their work in a way not enjoyed by their southern colleagues, possibly feeling less need to conform to a predetermined 'correct' position. We feel that this need to start from 'where we all were' may well extend the relevance of the book rather than confine it; there are recurring themes which should inform the practice of anyone working with Asian communities, and indeed with community development.

The three settings in fact complement each other, each concerned with a variety of issues, and each presenting a different emphasis. Cleveland demonstrates the workings of a community development section within a local authority department, and focuses particularly on the process of organisational and institutional change. Rochdale Community Project, an agency jointly managed by a national organisation and a local authority, provides glimpses of the costs, benefits and tensions involved in an organisational setting within or close to local government. The Al-Hilal project, a non-statutory project located in the Cheetham area in north Manchester, offers the opportunity to explore the relationship of a community organisation to the political life of the city. The issues of concern vary from group to group within each locality, and range from housing and environment, social and recreational facilities, to religious and cultural identity. Through all this run themes which concern the essence of community development: accountability, participation and power.

As the book emerged, it became evident that the initial remit would by and large provide a worthwhile study. Yet there were limitations to the initial concept, and the scope of the study grew naturally in a number of directions in order to fill gaps which were identified by the group, although it was always bound by resource restrictions. The writer brought to the project extensive experience of voluntary and community organisations as an organisation development consultant, and saw the need continually to place the particular detail within an analytical framework, and to look outwards from a purely local perspective at patterns between the regions and links with national trends, and with the political environment. The process was interactive, the writing emerging from some pre-existing written material, individual interviews and group meetings, the writer being in a position to take up, challenge or develop first-level analysis, or carry it and cross-refer between regions. One obvious move was to confront the male orientation of the original material produced. Changing this bias meant drawing in some additional material, contacting groups and individuals who had not been brought into the study at its early stages. Some groups were understandably reluctant to be brought in at what was felt to be a late stage, and limitations had to be recognised in our ability to cross-refer to other developments.

The process was a positive one for participants, as they found their own analysis both taken up and challenged, and indeed for most members of the core group, the experience was valued not so much as a writing exercise but as a process which offered a sharing of experience and support. However, there were frustrations involved in organising group meetings to discuss the drafts. The time-scale of the project was extended several times. The logistics of getting material and responses from busy workers 100 miles apart, while the Community Projects Foundation and the author were located 200 miles south, made the whole process very protracted. It was tempting at times for the author to take over responsibility for moving things along, but it was important and rewarding that that responsibility and ownership remained with the group as a whole.

Although it often felt as though the discussion focused on negative experiences, on mistakes, on the difficult and painful episodes, there is much which is positive about current practice described in the book. There have been tremendous advances made by many of the community groups operating in the areas of the study. Any increase in confidence and skill has often taken place against the thrust of socio-economic forces and would in the estimation of members of the groups themselves have been unlikely without the support of community workers. Any limitation on their work comes from the failure of their agencies to act appropriately, national and local government policies, particularly the strictures of government funding, central and local, rather than from any inherent difficulties in working in a multi-racial setting. Indeed, at the time of writing those funding limitations in many cases are threatening to stifle the very blossoming of confidence and activity described above. As for the workers, and their agencies, they have been through a rapid and sometimes painful learning process which has extended their flexibility and capacity to work effectively within a multi-racial society. That process can never be complete, but they are more aware of the important issues, and how to think them through, and that must be a beginning.

Community Development with Asian Communities Project Group

Acknowledgements

As well as drawing on the experiences of those who made up the group which initiated and developed this study, an invaluable contribution was made by others who offered their views and analysis. Our thanks go to the following community workers, local government officers, politicians and other members of the community:

Shirley Abbott, Teema Asadi, Mr Amin, John Bradwell, John Best, Sandra Bowness, Arif Chohan, Mary Foley, Frank Hanley, John Harris, Qurban Hassan, Ted Jackson, Maleha Khan, Jeff Ludden, Sheila Mallieson, Ann McGeever, Mike Martin, Stephen Moore, Surinder Nagra, Ann Pritchard, Kate Rae, Mr Sabharwal, Sally Shaw, Zahir Siddiqui, Dave Slater, Jean Tye, Kanta Walker and Hajra Yasseem.

Particular thanks go to Linda Grant of the Community Projects Foundation whose enthusiasm for the project did much to ensure that it became a reality.

List of Agencies

Rochdale Community Project (RCP)
RCP was formed in 1981 as a partnership between the Community Projects Foundation, Rochdale Metropolitan Borough Council and Rochdale Voluntary Action. Staff consist of a project director, senior community worker, six community workers, three administrators, and for a period, with MSC funding, a resource worker.

The project is managed by a management committee and council consisting of representatives of Rochdale Voluntary Action, local authority departments and the Community Projects Foundation.

The aims of RCP are to assist the urban renewal process within Rochdale Community Based Action Areas and tenant participation on council estates, by establishing and supporting strong, independent and effective organisations able to reflect the opinions and concerns of local people. This is seen as an essential part of revitalising the sense of identity and the morale of neighbourhoods.

Several of the neighbourhoods in which the project has worked house sizeable Asian communities.

Cleveland County Social Services Department
Formed on local government reorganisation in 1974, the department covers the four boroughs of Hartlepool, Stockton-on-Tees, Middlesbrough and Langbaurgh, Cleveland contains a total population of 559,900. The estimated number of Cleveland's residents of New Commonwealth origin is 10,000.

The former Teeside County Borough first employed neighbourhood workers within the social services department in 1972. This was in response to the poor social conditions existing within the inner areas of Middlesbrough. Since the early 1970s neighbourhood workers have continued to be deployed within communities where there is a perceived social need throughout Cleveland.

The need to work with ethnic minority communities in Middlesbrough was recognised in 1981 and a neighbourhood worker was appointed with a specific remit. A second post was created in 1986 with a brief to work with ethnic minority communities in other parts of Cleveland.

In 1985 Cleveland Social Services Department adopted a strategy on race following the establishment of a departmental working party. This strategy led to the appointment of an adviser (ethnic minorities) whose role is to aid the development of appropriate services to meet the needs of ethnic minority communities.

Manchester Community Development Section
Part of the social services department, it was formed when the department was established in 1971. Separate from casework, residential and day care services, the community development section is responsible for:

Encouraging and assisting people in communities to come together to identify common needs, helping them develop groups and organisations to meet these needs through a combination of mutual self-help activities and co-operation with the department, city council and other agencies to ensure that policies, practices and allocation of resources reflect and respond to these needs.
(Revised job description, November 1984)

Staffing in the section has grown over the years and in 1988 consists of over 30 posts, which include ten neighbourhood community development officers and four community development officers with a specific brief to work with Afro-Caribbean and Indian Sub-Continent groups.

Although some work had been carried out with black groups since 1974, a major increase in the scope of this work came about with the appointment of four section-11-funded community development officers in 1985. The social services committee approved a draft anti-racist policy in January 1988 which is subject to three months consultation with black staff, black groups and trade unions. This falls within the overall equal opportunities policy of the city council.

Al-Hilal Community Project
The project was formed in 1980 from a number of separate Muslim organisations in the Cheetham area of Manchester with the support of staff in the community development section of the social services department. The project grew out of earlier work done with community groups in Cheetham focusing on a campaign for a local community centre.

Funding was obtained in the form of an Inner City grant through Manchester City Council. The grant covered a full-time field worker post, a part-time administrative secretary, and part-time teaching hours for Urdu and Islamic studies.

The main aims of the project are to help Asian families in the Cheetham area with advice, information, community work support and educational activities. The management committee consists of representatives from Asian groups in north Manchester and from the social services and education committees of the city council.

List of Members of Project Group

In Cleveland
David Appleton worked as a social service neighbourhood worker. In 1981, as projects officer, he was team manager when Cleveland appointed its first Asian community worker.
Meena Kumari came to Cleveland as a neighbourhood worker from the London Borough of Camden. During the period of the study she became the department's adviser on ethnic minorities.
Sue Little has always been Cleveland based, and worked as a neighbourhood worker exclusively with white groups until the SSD's moves to work increasingly with ethnic minorities.

In Rochdale
Mohammed Habeebullah joined the local authority and was seconded to Rochdale Community Project in 1981 shortly after qualifying as a community worker. He came with views about the changes possible in the structure of Rochdale's Asian community.
John Hargreaves worked for many years as a community activist, then as a community worker before joining RCP in 1981. Together with Mohammed Habeebullah he pioneered co-working in the team. They described their early work in *Design for Living: The Making of a Multi-Cultural Community Centre* in 1986.
Peter Hirst worked as a youth and community worker and social services neighbourhood worker before becoming project director in Rochdale in 1981. It was his first experience of management and he became concerned that the lessons from his experience of managing a multi-racial team be widely publicised.
Hanif Malik had worked in Rochdale since the mid-1970s,

firstly with the Commission for Racial Equality, and then for the Housing, and Planning and Estates Departments. He had a well developed pattern of working and range of contacts when he was seconded to the project in 1981.

Peter Dale as a development officer with the Community Projects Foundation was responsible for the design and early implementation of Rochdale Community Project. Within CPF, he has taken a lead role in raising the profile of race-related issues.

In Manchester

Christopher Ensor worked for many years as a community worker in Manchester SSD's community development section and as principal officer of that section since 1980. He published an article 'Organising in a Multi-Ethnic Society' with others in 1982.

Mohammed Salam was a founder member of the Al-Hilal Project in Cheetham Hill, which was set up from representatives of local Muslim organisations. He became employed as a fieldworker for the project when funding was obtained through the city council in 1980. He is active in a number of different organisations in the area, including the UK Islamic Mission and the city council's race sub-committee.

List of Abbreviations

ACW   Association of Community Workers
CBAA Community Based Action Area
CEP   Community Enterprise Programme
CPO   Compulsory Purchase Order
CRC   Community Relations Council
CRE   Council for Racial Equality
CRE   Commission for Racial Equality, London
CPF   Community Projects Foundations
CRO   Community Relations Officer
GIA   General Improvement Area
HAA   Housing Action Area
KYP   Kashmir Youth Project
MPA   Muslim Parents' Association
MSC   Manpower Services Commission
RCP   Rochdale Community Project
RMBC Rochdale Metropolitan Borough Council
RVA   Rochdale Voluntary Action
SAA   Sparth Asian Association
SSD   Social Services Department

1 Agencies and Communities

Cleveland

Cleveland Social Services Department employs neighbourhood workers in a separate section to undertake community development projects in target areas throughout the County of Cleveland. It expresses its aims of neighbourhood work as consistent with the Seebohm Report of 1968;[1] wherein community development was seen as 'a process whereby local groups were assisted to clarify and express their objectives and to take collective action to attempt to meet them; it emphasises the involvement of the people themselves in determining and meeting their own needs'. The Seebohm Report also suggested that 'a sense of community may need to be promoted among people for whom it does not exist, whilst in recognisable communities, effort may be needed to preserve and strengthen common identity and activity'. In their concern for the gap between managers of services and consumers, the department's objectives also showed the influence of the dominant perspectives of the 1960s and 1970s, exemplified by the two Gulbenkian Reports of 1968[2] and 1973,[3] establishing workers in an interpreting and liaison role between agencies and communities.

This emphasis was seen in the job descriptions of neighbourhood workers in Cleveland, which identified working with individuals and groups of residents to identify local needs, and developing resources within neighbourhood communities, but also placed an emphasis on providing an information service 'within a community development framework' and on developing and maintaining relationships and liaising with statutory departments and other agencies in the county and borough councils.

It was within this context that proposals were formulated to

1

appoint a neighbourhood worker to work specifically with ethnic minority groups. There were a range of concerns which shaped those proposals. It became clear in the late 1970s that the department's expressed aims could not begin to be attained in relation to the ethnic minority groups in Central Middlesbrough without a special initiative. Information on the ethnic minority population and the needs of black people in the inner areas was sketchy, or non-existent, and attempts at involving black people in existing white community organisations had proved ineffective. From the outset the prospective community worker's role was defined in terms of departmental rather than community needs. Social services staff had expressed a need for language assistance and concern was also voiced at that time by the education department, which had recently opened a centre for multi-cultural education, that a disproportionate amount of staff time was being used in an advice-giving and interpreting role. This dual focus was reflected in the funding submission made in 1978 to the Inner Areas Programme for a Neighbourhood Worker (Ethnic Minorities).

Although acknowledging gaps in service provision, Cleveland SSD was looking outside its own service posts for solutions in terms of specialist assistance. With hindsight it could be seen that the 'solution' served to point up the failure of the initial premise and had the ultimate effect of moving the department towards consideration of more fundamental change. The post was to lose its more formal interpreting functions, but it will be seen that in its widest sense of go-between, such a role remained very much at the heart of the functions of the neighbourhood workers in Cleveland, perhaps most overtly in those demanded of the department's black workers.

The department's original perception of the neighbourhood worker's role, then, incorporated a strong emphasis on practical advice and interpreting needs and was matched to a large extent by the community's expectation of a local authority community worker. This was incorporated in the job description of the SSD's first neighbourhood worker appointed in October 1980 with a specific remit to work with ethnic minorities in Central Middlesbrough. Later attempts were made to limit this interpreting role as it became apparent that the need went far beyond what could be reasonably offered by the worker; however, advice work continued to be an important part of the function of the post.

A survey of the Asian population of Middlesbrough, carried out in the early part of 1982 by the county council's research and intelligence unit,[4] served to some extent to supply the missing social information. The survey found that in comparison with all residents in Middlesbrough, a disproportionate number of Asians, three quarters of whom were of Pakistani origin, were employed in the manufacturing industry generally and more specifically in the metal manufacturing industry.

As manual workers they were in a particularly vulnerable position in relation to the decline in heavy industry in the region. The unemployment rate for Asian men at 29.3 per cent was similar to that of the total male population in inner area wards. On the other hand, the Asian population, in common with that in Manchester and Rochdale, was young in composition, 51 per cent being under 16. The unemployment rate experienced by Asians born in the United Kingdom showed an appallingly high rate, 42.3 per cent, most of whom were school-leavers.

Housing conditions were similarly poor. A very high proportion of Asian households, 90 per cent, were owner-occupiers, with 26 per cent of these households living in overcrowded conditions. The survey also highlighted both the lack of knowledge within the community of existing service provision, and the clearly expressed desire for language classes, groups for women, activities for children and a separate Asian community centre. The survey revealed that 41 per cent of those interviewed had never heard of the social services department. The low take-up of services suggested that the department would generally have contact with individuals from the Asian community only where there was a statutory responsibility; the Asian community would have contact with the department only in extreme cases, thereby distorting perceptions by and of the agency. For their part, the conventional wisdom among social workers was that the Asian community 'look after their own'[5] and the appropriateness of the services offered was not questioned.

This generalised inaccessibility of services in an area of high unemployment and poor housing conditions was to be an important point of departure for neighbourhood work in Central Middlesbrough as it developed after 1984. In mid-1984 the third consecutive black worker was appointed to the Central Middlesbrough Project; a decision was taken that she would work together with a second worker in the area on the model of separate work with black and white communities, accompanied by some joint projects and joint responsibilities for the planning and development of the whole project. Their focus became increasingly the provision of more and appropriate resources and services to the community.

Rochdale

Following reorganisation of local government in Rochdale and the surrounding areas in 1974, it was decided to assess the condition of the borough's private housing stock. Nearly a third of Rochdale's housing was pre-1919, over 75 per cent of this owner-occupied, with overcrowding well above the national average. The inner areas of Rochdale had been neglected and even blighted for many years. The 1974 assessment identified 12,500 houses in 19 areas which in some way required improvement.

It was seen that the Council needed to demonstrate its commitment to those areas and 'to persuade and encourage residents to invest their money and energy in the future of their area'. An approach which looked to 'sensitive gradual renewal as an alternative to the disruptive effect of widespread demolition and total redevelopment policies' was developed into an area-based strategy of improvement. A local office and multi-disciplinary team, including environmental health and other council officers, was established for each area, to pursue house improvement, and to agree and implement a whole range of urban renewal activities.

Nineteen community-based action areas (CBAAs) were prioritised according to the degrees of stress experienced and a rolling programme was devised with work scheduled to begin in a new area every six months. It was intended that a variety of approaches should be used to tackle what were in the first four of five CBAAs, severe housing problems. A combination of general improvement areas (GIAs), housing action areas (HAAs) and environmental improvement schemes were therefore drawn up for these CBAAs, the first of which was activated in 1976.

The 'community based' title referred to the underlying rationale that in order to encourage people to play a part in the improvement of their locality by taking up improvement grants, and committing themselves to what in many cases were significant mortgage repayments, the council felt it important to promote a closer relationship with, and a more receptive attitude towards local communities. The strategy was also calculated to encourage the participation of residents in decisions affecting the improvement process and to 'rebuild neighbourhood morale', thus increasing the chances of improved areas being adequately maintained. Most importantly, the objective was to maintain residents in their existing localities; earlier slum clearance had given rise to considerable dispersal of communities across areas.

This policy applied particularly to the Asians of Rochdale, 95 per cent of whom lived in the inner core of Rochdale town itself. In 1985 Rochdale had a population of 95,000, 15,000 of whom were Asian families. At the time of RCP's arrival in Rochdale, census figures indicated that housing conditions for the Asian population were far worse than that of the rest of the population. This was in a situation where 30 per cent of all households in the borough were in receipt of supplementary benefit and the people of Rochdale showed a higher incidence of ill health than the national average. Fifty-six per cent of Asian households were overcrowded, a much higher rate than among the white population. Moreover, Asian men had been hard hit by the fast contracting textile industry; between 1978 and 1982, 35 per cent of full-time male jobs in textiles were lost. Most of the Asian men who arrived in Rochdale in the 1960s and 1970s came to work in the textile mills, usually on night shifts. By 1985 it was estimated that there was 35 per cent unemployment in the Asian community, borough-wide, with particularly high levels of unemployment in the inner areas of Rochdale.[6]

In order to undertake community work within CBAAs and to establish a closer relationship with members of the Asian community, three community workers were employed, two of whom were Asian, under section 11 funding.[7] It was also felt that additional specialist community development assistance was needed to fully implement resident 'participation'. The use of this term presents some difficulty. Community Project Foundation's definition of community development would appear to interpret participation as an effective and influential 'input of ideas from the community'. Most frequently what emerges in our areas of study is 'consultation' – essentially an exchange of information. There is often disagreement as to whether such public involvement in decision making involves any real transfer of power. In Manchester, in 1985 and 1986,

the city council was making attempts to grapple with the concepts of 'participation' and 'consultation' and their implications,
recognising that the words themselves were often used loosely
and interchangeably. Public participation, they argued, can take
place only where the public have real power in the formal
decision-making machinery; consultation as such contains no
such concession to power-sharing. The council emphasized the
need to be clear about the kind of involvement being sought and
offered. Yet such clarity did not always exist within the agencies
themselves, and even less between agencies.

In the early 1980s, then, Rochdale Metropolitan Borough
Council turned to Community Projects Foundation (CPF) to
augment and direct the borough's community work input. In
mid-1981, Rochdale Community Project (RCP) was set up by
CPF in partnership with the metropolitan borough council to
assist in implementing resident participation in its housing improvement programme. RCP found the CBAA programme still
operating in the inner areas of Rochdale; the rolling programme
had not moved forward as quickly as anticipated. Nevertheless
RCP was led to expect a short-term involvement in the last
stages of the CBAA programmes in the inner wards; in fact the
programmes did not close in those areas until 1985 and 1986,
and even then the withdrawal by RCP workers in those areas,
while much debated within the project team, was a gradual one.
One of the project's first tasks was survey work of some of the
inner areas of Rochdale, among them the wards of Milkstone,
Wardleworth and Sparthbottoms, which housed much of
Rochdale's Asian community. Joining the team at the end of that
year were two black workers seconded from the local authority.

CPF jointly funds and manages community work in
partnership with local authorities. It expresses its perspective
in the following way:

The aim of community development is not to compete with the public
administration but to enable them to relate more closely to community
life, whilst helping community activities themselves to become more
confident, effective and influential. A CPF view of community development therefore envisages changes both in the community and in
public agencies, within the framework of representative democracy.

In CPF's judgement, a community development project will be
most effective if it is linked to the local authority but not part of it. The
project needs to have an identity which is felt, by local residents, to be
informal, unthreatening, 'on their side'. It needs, at the same time to

be clearly sanctioned by the local authority, to have a regular channel for feeding its findings back to the authority, and for gaining access to officers at all levels to facilitate the input of ideas from the community. Ultimately there will be positive action and a sense of joint achievement.
(Community Projects Foundation, 1985, pages 7 & 8)

The Rochdale invitation offered an opportunity to CPF to work closely with a local authority which recognised the value of gaining the views and enlisting the support of residents in the renewal of their communities. The fact that the local authority additionally saw community work as having a key part to play in this process, recognised some of the risks and was apparently prepared to accept criticism was an essential element in laying the foundations for CPF involvement.

Rochdale Community Project was set up jointly by Rochdale Metropolitan Borough Council (RMBC), CPF and a third partner, Rochdale Voluntary Action. It was soon apparent that RCP offered a serious challenge to the local authority view of community development, which had much in common with that of the Cleveland SSD. Participation was seen as a way of improving the performance and responsiveness of local government. The officers based in CBAAs were not community-work trained and were involved in community activities in a highly participative, and directive way. They operated not to defined strategies, but as 'well-intentioned innocents' according to one council officer. RCP's objective, by contrast, went beyond responsiveness to partnership: to move away from what were perceived as 'safe' areas of involvement to work within a strictly limited timescale with residents to help define objectives and to assist organisation and negotiation with the authority. Official response to RCP's intervention was not always enthusiastic, one council officer commented wryly: 'like a magical touchstone, the worker moved on once the way forward was revealed to residents'.

For RCP the desired position was an 'arms length relationship' in which the workers could be involved in situations where they could be critical of local authority practice; in practice the agency was required to exercise sufficient restraint to allow it access and influence, although there were occasions when RCP found it had crossed the indistinct boundaries of acceptable criticism and moved into apparently dangerous areas. For the council there were advantages. Not only were chief officers offered an alternative perspective often blocked from them by their middle managers, but they were able to gain knowledge and warning of potential flashpoints in the community in relation to policy.

Manchester

A 1986 Manchester City Council report on poverty in Manchester[8] showed up the results of the dramatic increase in unemployment since 1978, affected most severely by the decline in manufacturing, the traditional employment base of the city. In October 1985, 45,700 Manchester residents were unemployed, nearly a quarter of the workforce. Taken together with estimates of the large numbers of wage earners on 'poverty wages', about half of all Manchester residents were found to live below the poverty line. The more than doubling of unemployment figures in the first half of the 1980s meant that by 1985 nearly a third of Manchester residents were on supplementary benefit. Unemployment figures for the inner city were the most dramatic, one in every three men being unemployed, the brunt being borne by young people. Statistics indicated that well over half the young men were out of work in the city, official figures showing male unemployment as higher than that of female.

The report provides no figures relating specifically to black communities in Manchester. Indeed it provides an immediate comment on the services offered by the SSD, that its community development section has no access to, nor is it able to locate, up-to-date, substantive data which would provide precise information on the socio-economic or housing conditions of black communities, or their access to health and other welfare services. Yet the outline information in the profile of black communities by the city planning department[9] undoubtedly places them in the forefront of those affected by economic decline and rampant unemployment.

Although there were earlier settlements of families from the Indian sub-continent following the upheavals caused by the partition of India and Pakistan in the immediate post-independence period, the main movement of Indian and Pakistani men to work in Manchester industry was throughout the 1960s, their families joining them in the following decade. At the 1981 census the Pakistini community was the largest in number, and the third largest ethnic minority group in Manchester. By that date it was already a young population, over 70 per cent of the population of Pakistini-headed households being under 30, with a high proportion (16.5 per cent) of under-fives. The population in households where the head was born in India, East Africa or Bangladesh similarly contained high proportions of children, although the differences between this and the population in UK-headed households were not so marked. It was these same young people who were to meet the sharp edge of unemployment in the mid-1980s.

Pakistani households are concentrated in three main areas in inner Manchester: Cheetham Hill in the north, and in Longsight and Whalley Range, south of the city centre. Indian, East African and Bangladeshi families are more dispersed throughout the city, but live mainly in South Manchester and Cheetham. In 1978 the National Dwelling and Housing Survey on housing conditions and population structure in England designated Manchester as a housing stress area, and indicated that the Asian population was living in the areas of poorer housing where basic amenities such as a bath were either lacking or shared. Over 70 per cent of the Asian sample were owner-occupiers and a fairly high population of Asians lived in the private furnished rented sectors.

There were significant differences between the areas. In Whalley Range in 1985, an area with very little council rented housing and a substantial private rental sector, the population showed evidence of movement out to other wards, the population of the ward as a whole falling by almost 6 per cent. There was a significant fall in the number of young children, and there were large numbers of young single people living alone or together, a quarter of the ward's population being aged between 15 and 24 years. Longsight Ward also showed a declining population of 5 per cent between 1981 and 1985, with significant decreases in the numbers of children, including a fall in the 0–4 years age group, whereas the number of under-fives across the city increased by 20 per cent.

Cheetham, an inner city ward to the north of the city centre, with a long history as a transition area, contrasts vividly with this picture. Extensive redevelopments since the Second World War had caused major movements of population throughout the city. Immigrant groups in the 1960s and 1970s came from the Punjab and Mirpur districts of Pakistan, and moved into the remaining areas of terraced housing. A number of community facilities were lost in the mid 1970s as a result of redevelopment, including a secondary school, a further education centre, a library and swimming baths, a mosque and a Sikh temple. In the years 1981 to 1985 the population of Cheetham increased by 12 per cent, whereas the number of the people in the city fell by around 2.15 per cent, with the 0–4 years age group increasing by 32 per cent, well above the city average. In the 1985 poverty survey Cheetham showed up as one of the areas of highest unemployment, about 31 per cent, and showed in the highest group of private households receiving housing benefit who were also receiving certificated supplementary benefit.

In 1978 an application was put forward by a Muslim group for Inner Areas Funding for educational work, particularly for mother-tongue teaching, and for recreational and youth work. The members of the group which eventually became the Al-Hilal Project were closely associated with the community development section of Manchester SSD. It became evident that separate premises were required, and a funding application was put forward. It was three years before the application was successful; by then the grant submission was halved because of intervening government cuts. In January 1981 the newly established Al-Hilal Community Project appointed a community worker to develop its advice, education and youth work with the Muslim community, and to liaise with statutory bodies and voluntary agencies in the area. That staffing of one full-time community worker and part-time administrative assistance was increased in 1982 by MSC funding, bringing to the project a youth worker and an interpretation/liaison worker.

A changing political environment
Harry Blagg and Nick Derricourt put forward the following proposition:

What is obvious is that community workers have lacked a well-developed and articulated conception of the state and their own position on its margins. We believe that, on the whole, radical community work practice has been informed by a view of the state which tends either to divorce the state altogether from problems of the community or to reduce it to its capitalist repressive structures.
(1982, page 17)

We would argue that workers in this study may not have worked to a well-defined theory of state and community, but were empirically only too aware of the effects of a declining economy spiral and of the interface between local and national politics and policies and community action. As early as 1981/1982 heavy protests were registered in Rochdale against the Department of the Environment's wholescale disregard for all schemes put forward for grant aid under the Urban Aid Programme in favour of local authority schemes. There were several occasions when funding decisions cut at the very heart of community action. Furthermore, between 1981 and 1984 notions of equal opportunities were being developed within local authorities; at the same time there was a development of black community groups. Community development contributed to and was affected in an important way by both and by the interaction between the two.

In the opinion of many in Rochdale, neighbourhood politics throughout the period was dominated by the personality and style of the Liberal MP, although the borough council witnessed shifts in party political control. In May 1982 the Labour Party had lost power to a Liberal/SDP/Conservative alliance on the borough council. This changed in mid-1986 when the Labour Party regained power. Labour activists had begun moving into the same community networks previously explored by the Liberal Party, and the Labour Group now held a clear majority on the council.

One consequence of the political change was a new council overtly more 'race relations' conscious than its predecessor. However, this had contradictory consequences. The council's equal opportunities policy, formulated in 1981, remained without a code of practice or other defined strategy for implementation. On the other hand some practical measures had been made possible through the nature of the co-operative politics then current in the council's committees and sub-committees. The changed political realities of 1986 removed the rationale for co-operation; competition and political one-up-manship could operate effectively to defeat the passage of practical equal opportunity measures.

The 1986 election brought a lone black member on to Rochdale Council, and certainly no dramatic change of perspective. Moreover any effective black pressure through the race relations consultative bodies was effectively offset by political infighting. Developments in the other two areas of our study were scarcely more encouraging. One observer's comment was that within Cleveland County Council, there was a more overt movement away from previous equal opportunities initiatives following a shift to the right of the Labour Party by the controlling Labour Group in the county council election of 1985.

In Manchester the situation was more complex. The right-wing Labour Council which preceded the 1984 elections gave recognition but no priority to equal opportunities. The Labour Council which succeeded it in 1984 was avowedly anti-racist; however, what this meant in practice was a selective approval for race initiatives. Left-wing politicians had welcomed into the party the younger, more radical black members from South Manchester; they were less enthusiastic about certain others, perceived as operating under the patronage of the mosque elites, or some of the causes they espoused.

Meanwhile two conflicting trends were developing within Asian communities; on the one hand more people were seeing that it might be useful to affiliate to political parties and that there were practical advantages in terms of resources to be gained through party political channels, and sometimes the tactical use of parties and politicians. On the other hand, there was a growing belief by some young Asians both from the 'left' and the 'right' that such manipulation might at best be a two-way process, and one in which the politicians stood to gain most. These demands and changing awareness were inevitably reflected in the worker's experience of community development with those communities.

The Asian communities – divisions and loyalties
This exploitative edge to the relationship between party politicians and their black constituents can be seen mirrored in the attitude of local authority officers. The perception current in the 1970s of the Asian community, if not of the wider black population, was of a homogeneous whole. This view had legitimised dialogue with the community through key personalities, a process often reinforced through the community relations councils (CRCs) and councils for racial equality (CREs). Justified by, and reinforcing their own view, divisions within the Asian community could be used as a reason to withhold funding.

Politicians and council officers had in this way been shielded from recognising the realities of a highly structured traditional but pluralistic society which existed in the three areas. In each the majority of Asian households were of Pakistani background, although Wardleworth in Rochdale contained most of Rochdale's Bangladeshi population, and Cleveland's Indian community was located largely in outer Middlesbrough. A major proportion of all three Pakistini communities came from the Mirpur area of Pakistan. The rural Muslim majority of that area in the main lacked primary level education and basic literacy skills; they had transposed rigid social systems on to urban British society. Such organisation as existed in Rochdale and Cleveland, mainly religious and cultural, was dominated by an older generation of urban-based Punjabis, and few Asian youth or women's organisations existed. If there was an inherent latent conflict, in Rochdale where a challenge was put out for control of resources by younger Rochdale-educated Kashmiris, the conflict became overt.

In Cheetham Hill, where 90 per cent of the Pakistini community came from rural backgrounds, status difference was reinforced by class and economic factors, derived from their position in British society, and affecting leadership patterns, and social and religious life. Many small landowners who started off in Manchester in the 1960s as traders, later became wholesalers. This was the most traditional group which dominated the wealthy Central Mosque, drawing its office bearers from the business community. The second mosque in the area, led by urban-based professionals, drew its membership from low income groups and the unemployed manual workers. The conflict between the two mosques was an important part of the political life of the community.

In Rochdale, where a similarly high percentage of the Asian population were rural Kashmiris, the divide along urban/rural lines was also reinforced by economic and class difference. In both Rochdale and Middlesbrough those from rural backgrounds were employed as skilled and unskilled workers in the textile and metal industries; the leadership in both cases had been business or professional men, often urban-based Punjabis. In Rochdale at least there was to be a significant change in this pattern.

The importance of these factors varied from area to area. Sparthbottoms in Rochdale, for example, was small and isolated, and with no local mosque, there was little organised social or religious activity. In Wardleworth the urban/rural divisions were so strong that neighbours with those backgrounds were not talking to each other. The pattern of community development, the separate and often competing demands of communities in these areas in the first half of the 1980s, the realities of 'consultation', were to destroy the notion of the homogeneous 'community'. Those previous notions had been bureaucratically convenient; the mid-1980s found many local authorities struggling to 'safely' accommodate those altered perceptions within the constraints of local government spending cuts and their own dominant party political position on equal opportunities and anti-racism.

Consolidating the changes

In all three of our areas community development was concerned primarily with the relationship between community groups and power and resources. In relation to black communities, community workers were looking for change in three areas:

- real participation by black communities in the decision-making process
- altered perceptions of the views and aspirations of the black communities by the local authority members and officers, to reflect a multiplicity of needs and demands within and between communities
- improved quality and levels of service provided to black people and their involvement in the provision of that service

Such changes must be put in the context of notions of equal opportunities developing in local authorities in the early and mid-1980s; there was an inter-relationship between these initiatives and the development of community groups. Individuals working alongside those groups often experience the contradictory pull for developments in line with concepts of equal opportunities and multi-cultural resource provision as against the increasing reality of scarce resources, feeling themselves on the front line of the pressure to 'deliver the goods'.

David Thomas (1986, p. 33) claims that community work has been far more concerned with the vertical relationships of community groups to power and resource holders than to horizontal relationships of people and groups to each other. Indeed there would be some agreement that particularly for black groups struggling to gain resources there is a valid concern for the vertical, for access into the system. From a local authority perspective the appointment of black workers has certainly been seen in vertical terms, the purpose being to employ community development workers to work with groups who would then feed demands up through the system. In Manchester the role of the community development worker as laid down by the SSD was to give material assistance and support to organisations and groups to improve the quality of life. The role of the worker is seen as to inform, advise and enable the group to develop, and to gain more and appropriate resources. On the other hand this can be seen in a very real sense as a way of controlling community demands; one CRC member in the study comments, 'We are being contained.' Manchester City Council recognised there were particular problems for local authority community workers. If consultation or participation resulted in general agreement there was no problem, but where there was conflict between the council and the groups involved, it was easy for both sides to see the community development role as a manipulative one. Indeed vertical developments come into sharp focus in a depressed economy, as witnessed in the scarcity of resources at the local level. We will see that for the community development workers the lack of resources on offer can appear to call into question their very role.

In the design of RCP, too, it was very clear that workers were to organise residents' groups to influence the local authority, and it was this primary brief which sometimes, to the extent that residents expressed needs might indicate alternative action, created a level of conflict among workers as to priorities. On the other hand, in Rochdale we will see that in organising to gain control of that resource distribution, groups which were previously divided along tribal or urban/rural lines were sometimes brought together in a shared purpose. Indeed the experience of the workers in this study would indicate that while the horizontal relationships may be less visible, they necessarily inter-relate to vertical developments. Those inter-group relationships were indeed at times highly volatile; the process of public involvement itself sharpened other splits and conflicts.

This contradictory progress is seen elsewhere. In Manchester, although members of the two mosques engaged in sometimes violent conflict, they were able to unite around the issue of single sex education for Muslim girls. Indeed, the Al- Hilal community worker, although identified strongly with one mosque, and at times engaged in heady and violent conflict as a consequence, was recognised and used as a resource by the other in his advice functions and his link role with key agencies.

The consultative structures of the early 1980s served in many ways to highlight the difficulties which local authorities experienced in adjusting to the pace of community change and political pressure. There was also a difficulty in reconciling the demands of those consulted with their own ideological commitments. In Cleveland and Rochdale new community activists challenged the role of previous community leaders. In Manchester the CRC had been largely descredited before 1984, the Muslim population had not been well represented on it, and most dialogue was conducted in an ad hoc way with particular groups and communities. At the same time in all three areas, with the old umbrella organisations divided and discredited through power struggles, the councils created consultative channels, looking for more representative leaders. In Manchester, the setting up of the race sub-committee, set up after protracted negotiations in 1986, did to some extent bring in new activists, although some of the previously established leaders managed to retain their role.

The local authority community development sections in this study have remained largely outside and unconnected to this consultation process. In Manchester, for example, the section as a team wished to remain independent and unidentified with the politics of consultation. At the same time the view is expressed that had the council wished to give an effective voice to the neighbourhoods, or indeed had they recognised the advantageous position of community development workers, they might well have been brought within the process.

By contrast, in Rochdale RCP became heavily involved in the debate and in the shaping of consultation structures. The CBAA strategy and the community development process engaged in by RCP extended the whole principle of consultation to embrace many forms: formal and informal meetings with groups of residents, local seminars and finally the formation of area committees, in which residents could participate in formal council structures. In 1983, the chair of the CBAA sub-committee had submitted a report which recommended that the CBAA programme be reinstated as a priority; that there should be a corporate approach to urban renewal and a greater involvement of non-technical departments; and finally, that there should be a reorganisation of the way residents were involved.

In a direct line from these recommendations, in 1985 a joint RMBC/RCP initiative resulted in area committees being established in each of the active CBAAs 'to promote participatory democracy'. Serviced by the chief executive's department, and composed of councillors, council officers and residents, these were effectively council sub-committees with their own budgets and power to decide on issues of area improvement.

However, even with this extended principle it is worth considering the points made by Usha Prashar and Stan Nicholas (1986, p. 46). Only too often, they argue, the questions 'Why consultation?' and 'to what end?' do not appear to have been considered.

Because no clear thought was given to those questions, there has been substantial confusion about the objectives and the purpose of consultation. Consequently the 'who to consult?' has posed problems for local authorities. If the reason for consulting ethnic minorities is not clearly thought through, then the form of consultation rather than the contact may come to be seen as important. Such a situation creates an illusion that consultation is taking place, but it may not necessarily influence policy and practices in order to meet the needs of black and other ethnic minority communities; then the effective consultation arrangements are those which facilitate the direct expression of minority opinion to those in a position to bring about change. In this respect consultation does not refer to any one arrangement or just to formal arrangements, but to many activities by which those affected by the statutory services take some meaningful part in influencing policies and practices of local authorities.

How far this was achieved was dependent not just on the nature of the community itself or on community activities, but on the extent to which that process also had reference to inter-group relationships at a local level and the interaction between the worker and the agency on the one hand, and the community as part of the body politic on the other. Robin Hambleton and Paul Hoggett (1984) point out that 'decentralisation' can devolve 'authority' and 'influence'. Authority carries with it the ability to take action without prior confirmation from a higher level, while influence implies the ability to exert leverage on decisions affecting the neighbourhood. Although both are important, 'a common experience is that councils have been more successful in shifting the locus of influence as against the locus of authority'. (p. 2)

2 The Framework for Action

Evolution of workstyle

The community development worker's theoretical approach and analysis of the task at hand inevitably influences the nature of the intervention. Both in Rochdale and Cleveland, where community development work had direct contact with local authority structures, and in Manchester where the Al-Hilal worker had no formal channel of access to the local authority, there was a dual focus: on the one hand, on raising levels of consciousness and activity in the community; on the other, on confronting the sources of power.

In line with the assessment of needs, the Central Middlesbrough Neighbourhood Project initial work concentrated on an information and interpreting role. Information sessions were held at three centres and were widely used by the Asian community to gain information principally on welfare benefits and home improvement grants. In addition the sessions provided a first insight into the barriers that existed to the take-up of services. These were analysed in the following way:

• There was a lack of information and understanding of the structure and role of various agencies on the part of ethnic minorities.
• There was a lack of understanding of these difficulties on the part of the officers of these agencies.
• The situation was exacerbated by problems of language.

The opening of the Granville Road Community House in February 1983 offered the first step towards involvement in community activities. Emphasis in the early stage was placed on the development of youth provision through the junior club and the Asian boys' club. However, it was seen that groups catered for only a small sector of the community, and work remained predominantly with individuals. The neighbourhood worker was supported in this work by a neighbourhood work assistant, funded under the Community Enterprise Programme (CEP). As both workers were Asian men, some white residents saw the service as one exclusively for the Asian people in the area. It was felt that this perception of the community house would prejudice its objectives; when a second neighbourhood work assistant was recruited, the language requirement was dropped, and a white woman was appointed.

Although the CEP-funded neighbourhood work assistant scheme was terminated in 1984, this principle of joint working was pursued. The decision to allocate two neighbourhood workers to one project area was in part in recognition of the needs highlighted by the Asian survey and the size and complexity of the project area, but also because it was felt important that residents from both black and white communities perceived the Central Middlesbrough Project as being relevant to them.

The joint working enabled new initiatives to be taken. Among these were the development of contacts with smaller ethnic groupings; the Yememi and Somali populations of Middlesbrough, for example, had populations of 200 people or less. What also developed during this time was a joint understanding that it was necessary to focus on raising levels of understanding of racism, both in the black community and within the local authority and other agencies, and to emphasise the need for structural changes to counter inequalities.

Another prominent characteristic in Cleveland was that workers remained heavily engaged in work with individuals at a grassroots level. Although department community workers wanted to do more group work, their experience of it remained largely discouraging. The workers' analysis was that this was due to two factors: relatively undeveloped levels of political consciousness and lack of basic appropriate services. Where resources are minimal they feel, community workers are forced to respond to primary needs, and advice provision, for example is a tangible resource which people can identify and use.

If the Cleveland workers were in many ways caught within the parameters of the local authority conception of liaison, interpretation and meeting of needs, RCP was to all appearances, and felt itself to be, in an advantageous position. It defined issues in terms of community participation (see pp. 5–6 above) and representation of interests. Attention to methods of representation and negotiation with the policy-makers brought with it a direct interest in inequalities in the distribution of power. Indeed, for RCP one of the principal purposes of community development was to shift the relative degrees of power exercised by the local authority and local residents in favour of the latter: 'The people we work with are, by definition, living in neglected areas, have come to expect a low level of service and have been conditioned to have low expectations of their own abilities. Not surprisingly they are not usually optimistic about what the council can do for their areas.'

However, given that the central focus was the community, the emphasis was on enabling residents to be heard, by organising and presenting their interests in ways that would be acceptable to the local authority and to that extent there was less initial emphasis placed on changing the approaches and practice of the local authority than was the case in Cleveland, although that element was implicit. The difficulty lay with a basic premise which stopped short with an assumption of disadvantage, inarticulacy and low expectations by residents, and did not move squarely into an analysis of inaccessibility of services, inequalities and racism at the outset. Those realities were certainly acknowledged, and changes at this level were very much targets for community activity, but they were not written into area profiles, for example, and could not properly form the basis for action. The basic assumption was that such changes would take place as a result of community participation in decision making. One drawback to this is the underplaying of the resistance to change at an organisational level, the dangers of incorporation of community groups, and a tendency towards adaptation, rather than to real change. One RCP management committee member argues that even after five years of involvement in Rochdale, and high levels of credibility, RCP was not able to use its knowledge and material produced to best effect with the borough council because of its low-profile approach. There is evidently a question to be answered about the compatibility of high level political inputs and a grassroots approach to neighbourhood work.

Project workers would not necessarily put emphasis on the dangers of 'co-optation'. Although RCP perceives the council's functioning as remaining essentially paternalistic, there was a strongly felt commitment by officers to an active measure of consultation which in their view went well beyond seeking the views of residents and moved firmly towards shared decision making. Moreover, if by operating in some senses both as an agent of the local council and as an advocate of residents' interests, and in their own perceived community development role, they were precluded from directly confrontational tactics, they were nevertheless able to work with groups in a way which encouraged at times a critical response to council policies.

However, it is accepted that the development of area committees carried with it a risk of incorporation; indeed initially there was some feeling among residents' groups that they were no longer necessary, given the presence of area committees. RCP tried to maintain continuing independence by encouraging the maintenance of groups at the neighbourhood level, offering training in meeting skills and encouraging an active and creative approach to meeting agendas. RCP workers also saw that they had a valid role to change the way that officers operated in area committees, for example by persuading the council that they should not always expect to find a hierarchical structure of officers at meetings. One worker also argues for a measure of realism: 'You cannot continually hurl people over the barricades. Council does hold all the power and you have got to get in there and start changing attitudes from within. What you have to do is to retain enough of the confrontation so that you can show up that the group is not acquiescent or complacent.'

At one level RCP's objective involved understanding how residents perceived and experienced the council's actions, then increasing residents' knowledge of how local authorities work, what their rights were, and how to apply pressure in pursuit of their objectives. The local authority also needed assistance in being more open about the planning process and establishing channels for continuous as opposed to intermittent dialogue with the residents. But at another level it was a matter of actually altering the structures of decision making so that residents' wishes and opinions carried greater weight than before. To the community workers it sometimes felt as if RMBC was only committed to the first, limited level of community development, not to giving residents an increased role in policy making. In some CBAAs, where the council had set up offices and encouraged residents' groups, RCP workers believed that council officers were listening to only a few easily available, out-of-touch members of the community, whilst fostering a close relationship with other residents, which inhibited res-

idents from developing community identity, independence and a
critical perspective on the council's work.

The council's stated intention was to encourage residents to
become aware of the improvement programme and to express
their opinions and concerns in an effective manner so that they
might feel part of the overall process. It was clear to RCP that
there would on occasions be areas of contention and potential
conflict with the local authority which would arise when opinions and concerns were expressed; this was not a position
which was apparently shared by RMBC.

The council's harmonious model of community development
was reflected in the role assigned to the local authority community workers. RCP expected its workers to hand on
knowledge and skills which would enable residents to handle
politically sensitive issues. The weight of the council secondees' job description, by contrast, was on their feedback role
to the local authority, translating where appropriate, above all
interpreting needs and providing information 'on matters relating to ethnic minority groups'. The fact that some of the RCP
workers were council secondees and were permanent
employees of the planning department may well have operated
to make it more difficult for them to become involved in contentious areas.

Indeed, the question of approach was an important issue in
the team, and there was a difference in personal style which
only partly derived from the differing employee relationships.
Indeed, one of the white council secondees was able to take an
openly critical stance in relation to the council, which was not
seen to the same extent in the work of the black workers. It is
difficult to know in this situation where factors which relate to
power relationships and personal inclination overlap or are
self-reinforcing.

There may well have been other factors present which prevented a more active or critical stance which was not always
apparent or made explicit. For example, a report was drawn up
in mid-1982 based on evidence given by Asian householders of
poor building standards and inadequate response by housing
officers. Yet it was never acted upon by the Sparth Asian
Association to whom it was entrusted for action; a few individual
cases were taken but not pursued with legal action. How important was it that the complaints had been made by individuals
standing outside the mainstream of the Asian community, how

important the failing momentum within Sparthbottoms as a CBAA, how important the agenda of the community worker working with the association?

This did not mean that the boundaries of community action were not sometimes tested in work with Asian groups. In 1982 the housing group, attached to Wardleworth Community Association, whose membership was predominantly Asian young men, submitted a report to the CBAA sub-committee. The report pointed to a general lack of an educative approach to using the system and management of building work, and to the inability of the CBAA office to provide the kind of help which residents needed, leading to inadequate information about the grant system and substantial problems with building standards and practice. It was pointed out that these shortcomings were not helped by the fact that technical staff were unable to speak to residents in their own language.

The relationship between RCP and RMBC was thus a potentially precarious one. Given that resources were at the heart of the partnership, it is not surprising that their threatened removal should point that up. When cash for improvement grants and environmental improvement money was drastically cut back after the General Election of 1983, it appeared to undercut the very rationale and basis for the relationship with the council. For RCP the whole purpose behind RCP's style was that the council had money for a given area and that they organised groups to help them to spend it more effectively on things the residents considered important. If the residents' trust in RCP's ability and knowledge were now shaken and the council's credibility with residents had disappeared in some areas of work, then, as one worker put it to the management committee: 'If the partnership model is no longer appropriate we are likely, as we continue to work in CBAAs to encourage groups to adopt a more progressive campaigning style.' However, there was concern that there were already signs of scapegoating of Asian residents and although there were some members of the management committee who would have welcomed a move towards a more campaigning style, this was not a view uniformly held.

The nature of accountability

RCP declared a first-line responsibility and responsiveness to the local community, but this was not where effective accountability lay. This was reflected and in part derived from

RCP's management structure. In the course of this study one response to discussion in this area was that 'community accountability is a tired subject which does not need to be aired yet again'. Indeed, it is a familiar debate within community work, but nevertheless an issue which remains contentious; it must also be asked whether there are particular issues raised by work with Asian communities.

Discussion is not assisted when the meaning attached to terms is unclear. Accountability or 'calling to account' contains an element of control; this normally lies with the employer and managing body, whereas community accountability is more accurately an answerability, or sense of moral obligation and of conduct being influenced by discussion. These are different notions and each require mechanisms to be effective; there is a question to be asked as to whether it is necessary to formalise the process of answerability and responsiveness into mechanisms of control. The Cleveland neighbourhood workers, for example, felt that they necessarily worked within clear lines of accountability to the local authority which employed them. At the same time they felt it important to avoid attempts by community leaders to control their actions; responsiveness must involve freedom to interpret between often competing demands.

For the community worker employed by a community organisation the lines may not appear so clear. The Al-Hilal worker was required to operate within the framework of the hopes, expectations and demands of his organisation's membership, while being accountable to a management committee which was made up of what appeared at times to be irreconcilable interests: community representatives, councillors and council officers. On the one hand he frequently felt compelled to act on his own perception and interpretations, unable to stay at the same level as the community he was working with, while effectively he felt constrained by the local authority which funded him. He was expected by the authorities to be able to express an authoritative opinion. This was reinforced by the expectation of the management committee that he would give a clear lead. What was required in this situation was conscious attempts to create channels for real accountability to the management committee and for partnership with community activists.

It was in part a pressure on him by the community itself, an expectation that he was paid to act on their behalf, and in part a more general lack of understanding about a community work role which prevented the worker from creating that accountability. This was reinforced by pressure to achieve results within a short time period, and his high profile engagement in other networks, such as the Labour Party and the Mosque. In campaigning against the local authority for single sex education for Muslim girls, local Muslim parents wanted him to take a front-line position, while the management committee pulled him back. Helping him to face what the worker describes as 'unbearable tensions', the city's principal community development officer, previously a worker in Cheetham, in the worker's words 'watched, guided and helped me'. Encouraged on the one hand to assist rather than lead action, in line with community development practice, he would pull back at times from a predominantly front-line position. However, perhaps inevitably, it was the salary rather than the role which was perceived by some individuals in the community as the obstacle. He remembers the reaction from the Muslim Parents Association with which he was working: 'Something is holding you back and you are betraying us for the few thousand pounds you are getting from the council.'

For such workers, often isolated, this raises the question of the role of a support group without the functions and vested interests of the management committee; at the very least there is a need to include funding for consultants and trainers in project budgets.

RCP had consciously placed itself within an elaborate structure of checks and balances which, designed to promote access upwards into the local authority departments through the co-option of key officers, at the same time excluded resident control. Team members were accountable to the project director, who in his turn was accountable to the management committee; a project council acted as a formal second tier. The three partners which came together to form the management committee and the project council were RMBC, CPF and Rochdale Voluntary Action (RVA).

RCP's relative independence from the council had not been self-evident within such a structure and, aware of the dangers of direct accountability, the issue had been fought out at an early stage. In a letter to CPF in 1982 the project director had argued that while we recognise the need for input from and communication with elected members and officers we are not a council department and should not be directly accountable. Residents' associations and community groups with whom we work can only perceive our role as credible if we are independent of direct control by the borough, and of the service provision departments who report to the CBAA sub-committee. Similarly we would hope not to be exposed directly to control or influence by one or other political party, which may become a possibility in a council committee.

A wider accountability was in fact argued to the extent that each partner was accountable to its parent organisation which was in its own way accountable to a wider constituency. The stated intention was that the detailed agenda must be 'determined by the people with whom we work and that it would be inappropriate and largely unworkable for either workers or management to overimpose their views on the direction of the programme'.

Black communities, white management

There was no doubt that the objective of improving communications between RCP and the local authority service departments was very largely met. The management committee achieved a high level of commitment from its local authority members, as well as the promotion of RCP's independent status, which proved useful at times when this was challenged.

However this did not minimise the very real concern about the absence of black people and women in the management structures, expressed particularly by RVA. RVA had been involved in the community-based action areas action forum to pressurise RCP for better resident involvement in the project's management, an aim which it feels has not been met. The only attempt to get a woman involved in the committee failed because of the unsuitability of meeting times to her childcare needs and in the opinion of one member, 'there was never a serious attempt to get black committee members'. The result was a committee which was white, male and professional in character, an atmosphere which was, he believes, discouraging or oppressive to staff, and rendered it almost invisible to the community. One worker admits, 'we recognised the inconsistency of encouraging groups to have more control over council departments, whilst being unaccountable to them ourselves', although he himself had argued at the time in a paper to the committee: 'Few residents with leaking roofs and rotting window frames would be prepared to spend less time on sorting out those issues so they might indulge in the luxury of managing a community worker.'

There may have been a real problem in finding a way of having a management committee which was accountable to the community and involved the principles already established. There seemed to be two issues. One concerned the purpose and style of the committee. The second was that black people and women in particular were excluded from representation. The problem was that if RCP remained committed to a committee which prioritised links into the local authority, it seemed to wrap up the argument for the representation of those groups until such time as they were in positions of power in the borough.

However, this lack of community representation in an agency's management structures has several consequences, and they are particularly acute in white-managed agencies working in multi-racial neighbourhoods. The first is that workers themselves decide residents' needs and interpret them to those in a management or supervisory role. This may be an uphill struggle, but whether they meet with support or opposition, to the extent that both reactions might be the product of lack of information, the result is necessarily a difficult if not untenable one for the worker. Neither accountability nor support can flourish in such conditions. As important is the probable lack of an integrated strategy for work based on a diagnosis which relates to the needs of a multi-racial area. In both Cleveland and Rochdale there was an acknowledgement by white managers that they lacked information on Asian communities; indeed part of the specific remit of the Central Middlesbrough neighbourhood worker was to collect and supply that information. Yet there was no recognition of the need to use that information itself to define the nature of community development work within those contexts.

A woman involved in community development in South Manchester in the early 1970s reflects on the experience of an Asian workers' co-operative which proved unable to develop the radical form in which it was originally conceived. The white members of its church-sponsored management committee, she argues, were unable to use the relevant information which existed in a dynamic and challenging way. In her view they were concerned about offending the interests of Asian businessmen, and opted for a three-year research project to look at employment patterns, although it was largely known that 90 per cent of the women were homeworking.

Having established and working later in a women's aid centre, she says:

Although my support structure were very well meaning, I felt that they could not share that kind of emotional level with me, and the types of pressures I was under which came from the kind of communities I was working with and whose expectations of me were very different. Nor did they have the empathy, the depth of understanding, and sometimes they were politically naive.

In this instance the worker also felt that the Church management committee had a naive approach to leadership within the community, believing that contact with businessmen would be sufficient to pave the way for the community worker.

There may be particular problems for Church bodies; the worker felt that when brought up against alternative cultural and religious perspectives, there were anxieties and concerns about intervening in people's lives. But community development 'is about intervening in people's lives'. The general point must be the inherent contradiction in a management committee made up of people who have boundaries around what they can do which are inconsistent with the real needs of the communities in which they are working.

Beyond the ability of management committees to provide appropriate support and direction there is also an important dimension which relates to the denial of opportunities to black people to manage community affairs. There is often a perpetuation of the stereotype in which white people are seen as managers, providers and policy makers and black people as receivers, and white agencies are often unable to perceive and reflect on this reality. Also delayed is a confrontation with the issue of whether white agencies are prepared to make resources available to black groups 'without strings attached'.

Whereas in Cleveland there was a *de facto* acceptance of the black worker's interpretation of necessary strategy (leading to an acceptance of quite different positions as put forward by different workers), in Rochdale the project fell back on an understanding of good community work practice, and the specific objectives of the project and acceptance of changing practice emerged only after a long process of conflict. What did not occur in either case was an integrated attempt to look at the needs highlighted by work with black people and multi-racial communities and to assess the basic premise of the project in that light.

A basic problem lies with an inability to take into the project design considerations of how, when and where racism affects communities, and how the agency will work with such a central and determining factor. As Basil Manning and Ashok Ohri point out, there is a general lack of guidance from academics or professionals on possible methods: 'The issue of racial prejudice, let alone racism, is still treated as marginal by community workers.' (Ohri, 1982) David Thomas enlarges on this point:

But in the issue of black participation, the community worker has both to deal with the broad issues of racial prejudice, disadvantage and institutional racism, and to devise his intentions in such a way as to support the membership of black people in community groups. In other words, the issues of white racism and black participation give community workers a structurally determined problem that is amenable to intervention and some change at local level. (1986, p. 32)

In Rochdale the area profiles were written before the two black workers joined the project. Yet it was on the basis of the profiles that the area objectives were based. In the Wardleworth Area Profile it was stated that it was not possible to examine the complex system of values and traditions held by Asian groups, nor attempt anything but a superficial assessment of their activities. The vagueness of the objectives drawn up for Milkstone betrayed the corner they found themselves in. They read:

The team feels that further time is required to take some action research to assess the extent to which residents identify with Milkstone CBAA and the strength of community networks within the area. The style of work that is envisaged would enable the team to pursue issues as they arise and this may involve the subsequent formation of interest groups.

Racism as such was not mentioned in the objectives for any of the areas; indeed consistent with the preoccupation with vertical relationships with the local authority there was no reference to inter-group work or relationships between ethnic groups.

Ranjit Sondhi, writing of the Asian Resource Centre in Birmingham notes that while it was obvious that Asians, in common with all other people who have to live in an impoverished inner-city area, experienced problems with housing, unemployment, education, social services and welfare benefits, those problems for Asians assumed a specifically racial dimension. 'It was the racism endemic at all levels in this society that magnified within Asian communities all the processes connected with working-class communities in decay.' (Sondhi, 1982)

As one worker pointed out, the white working-class communities with whom community development agencies concentrate are normally suspicious of the middle-class council employees. The black communities had every reason to be even more so given the presence of racism. When RCP started in Rochdale there were six Asian workers out of several thousand employees working for the local authority; black people were unlikely to see the local authority as being there to serve their needs.

Yet, although conscious of such facts, RCP's strategy and working methods were not informed by such considerations. For example, in Sparthbottoms, the decision by the two workers to encourage the formation of a separate Asian association arose as the only practicable solution to the situation they found in the Asian community: its non-involvement in the existing residents' association, its lack of English and its very different needs and demands. Although the workers were committed to improving communication and extending contacts between residents, they encouraged support for a multi-racial community centre because it was what the overwhelming majority of residents wanted rather than because of their own ideological position. Indeed separate development and resources was a more acceptable concept at that time. Once it was clear that the centre would be built, it was certainly their hope that it might serve as a forum where white and black people got to know one another better and learned to see each other in a less stereotyped way. But the community workers did not see it as their business to promote either social integration or cultural accommodation beyond what the residents themselves wanted.

RCP would argue that it would not have been possible to put the tackling of racism directly on the agenda at the outset, from the point of view of the working relationship with both the council and within the communities. Their early approach was that if racism came up as an obstacle to achieving goals, then this would provide an opportunity to work on it. Indeed team members can pinpoint many learning opportunities in their work with residents' and community associations and street level groups; they would point to a new and very real sense of co-operation and mutual understanding in areas such as Wardleworth and Sparthbottoms. Finally, the project was able in its renegotiations with the council to locate racism as a legitimate area of direct concern. Yet if that early approach to tackling racism was essentially a strategic one, that should not in itself have hindered an articulation of that strategy or the development of a joint understanding of racism; there could have been an explicit strategy which still started 'from where the residents were'.

One result of not having an explicit strategy was that there was little basis for discussion between team members. There were undoubtedly differences of approach and method but the basis for evaluation had not been satisfactorily established. Further, there was no real consideration given to where the power lay within the community as a whole. This meant, for example, that it was difficult to recognise that behind multi-racial community action in Sparthbottoms the Asian community were often reluctant to speak out and express their needs, and were fearful that the relationship with the white community might be jeopardised.

At the same time the white community resented separate and successful Asian activities; when the Sparthbottoms Asian Project came up for renewal the chair and management committee of the residents' association pushed for activities of both black and white groups to combine under one project head. A failure to recognise the elements in this move meant that there could be no effective strategy. This did not mean that there was no recognition of white racism in Sparthbottoms. Indeed, both workers were vigorous in challenging racism within groups and in writing to the press, particularly in relation to damaging media coverage of Asian community developments. In the Wardleworth area as well the workers feel they spent a con-siderable time with the white residents' association, attempting to change perceptions, despite a priority to develop young black leadership in the area.

It was precisely a focus on racism which provoked Cleveland

neighbourhood workers to concentrate on change within agencies in terms of their service to black people. Much of the work done with groups in Rochdale had a parallel aim. But RCP's inability seriously to discuss racism or to develop an anti-racist strategy in its early phase of work is a vital one; the issue was not raised by RCP until much later discussion on possible anti-racist work on council estates. We are brought back to our earlier consideration of the importance of the original premise and definition of priorities in determining the relationship of the agency to the community and the institutions of power. There must be a basic contradiction for both the black and white workers working with black communities where the nature of racism, both internal and external to the organisation, has not been discussed, nor a strategy agreed.

3 Participation or Power: The RCP Model

The RCP approach to community development requires people to recognise that they share a common problem and to decide that they want to tackle it. The aim of such a process is not only that the group should be in a better position to achieve its objectives at the end, but also that if a future problem or need were to arise, its members would be in a better position to handle it, having learnt re-usable skills.

The importance of the process, familiar to community development workers, was nevertheless not seen in the same way by Rochdale Council officers. Differences between RCP workers and CBAA officials centred on what RCP considered to be an overdirective approach to community work by council officers. Groups needed to work at their own pace, RCP would argue. If council officers were seen to take the lead in consultation, or to take over a group's idea, it could be confusing and demoralising for the people so far involved. To the extent that residents might be persuaded that the council had taken an issue on board or had taken a decision on it, then it would discourage the group from taking further action.

Ironically, this debate between certain council officers and RCP workers was paralled by a related one within RCP. If groups needed to develop at their own pace, might not their profile in the course of that development look very different according to the needs of residents and areas? If that were so, should the involvement of the community worker be determined by some externally imposed model or would it have to be determined by the nature of the groups themselves? The work with communities in Wardleworth, Sparthbottoms and Milkstone in the early 1980s was to make such issues the subject of sometimes heated debate within the team.

Sparthbottoms

Located close to the town centre of Rochdale, concentrated in the valley of the River Roch, Sparthbottoms is bounded on two sides by main roads and lies between the gas works on the eastern side and industrial properties to the west, with waste ground to the south and the river to the north. Its skyline is dominated by disused mills, gasholders and the town blocks of the town centre.

Because of the natural boundaries, Sparthbottoms gives the impression of being an easily identifiable community, isolated from others, and largely hidden from view. In the mid 1970s the future of Sparthbottoms as a residential area looked grim. It had been officially allocated to industrial use and there was a relatively high throughput of industrial traffic within the area. Many of the streets and houses, mostly built before 1914, and much of the surrounding land and buildings were in a state of marked disrepair.

Many elderly residents had died or moved out of the area, many complaining of the absence of a through bus service, of being cut off. When Sparthbottoms was declared a CBAA in 1978, there were about 32 industrial firms employing more than 700 people. There was a concentration of employment in engineering and significant numbers were employed in gas and construction industries as well as in textiles. The following years saw a deepening recession in the economy characterised particularly by a decline in the older manufacturing industries, including textiles and engineering.

Asian residents, some 60 per cent of the population, besides sharing in the general material and social deprivations, were – in the perception of the community workers – further disadvantaged in certain crucial respects: lack of English and unfamiliarity with British systems of government, administration and participatory democracy. A survey carried out amongst the Sparthbottoms Asian community in 1984 showed that 80 per cent of the heads of households arrived in the period 1961–70, whilst most wives, children and other dependents arrived in the following decade. Ninety per cent of the householders were owner-occupiers and 50 per cent were unemployed. Only a tiny fraction were fully competent in English and only half were literate in Urdu. So far as improving communication and extending contacts between the residents were concerned, it was soon apparent to the community workers that they would be starting virtually from scratch. In addition to a sharp division between the mainly elderly white and younger black residents, there was a marked absence of a sense of community in both sectors of the population, each being fragmented in various ways.

These were to be important considerations for the two RCP workers, one black and one white, who were allocated to work jointly in Sparthbottoms. When they started in the area at the end of 1981, material improvement work was already underway. But many Asian houses were still to be improved and the condition of the roads and pavements were poor. The major outstanding job was the reclamation of the open space between Sparthbottoms and the river which became an impassable swamp in the winter months. The material and social problems of the area provided an obvious focus for action which might overcome the barriers separating neighbour from neighbour. The residents' association had not been able to provide that impetus; it was chaired and dominated by an ex-mayor and ex-Labour councillor and alderman and negotiations were conducted directly between him and the local authority officials. The workers believed this to be an example of how a 'cosy' relationship had inhibited residents from developing community identity, independence and a critical perspective on the council's work.

Increased involvement was initiated through leafleting the whole area to ensure increased attendance at the AGM of the existing residents' association. A further objective was identifying ways in which the Asian community could meet its own priorities and become involved, where appropriate, in the association. The residents' association remained dominated by white residents who were unable to appreciate the problems faced by the Asian community. The agenda for the two groups was completely different: white people had already improved their houses, whereas for Asians the important issues concerned unsatisfactory standards of building work, problems with contractors, with environmental health officers and immigration cases. It was not surprising that the Asian residents were unable to appreciate the role of voluntary pressure groups, let alone the white-dominated residents' association, and were largely pessimistic about achieving successful solutions to their problems.

It also quickly became apparent that there were no Asian

institutions in Sparthbottoms, and residents, if they wanted to become involved in collective activity, were compelled to travel to Spotland or Milkstone. The black worker found that in order to gain credibility with the community he was obliged initially to take on a heavy load of individual problems, many involving translation and interpreting, related to housing, the DHSS and immigration.

In undertaking casework he encountered a considerable amount of scepticism from his co-worker in Sparthbottoms as to whether such work would lead to community action. The next move was to come up against criticism from local authority officers. A second leafleting of the area was followed by discussions with a number of local residents, and the Sparth Asian Association (SAA) was formed with the twin objectives of initiating collective Asian organisations in Sparthbottoms and disseminating information and encouraging discussions amongst Asians about the improvement programme; formal links were developed with the residents' association. It was decided that much of the liaison work with the Asian association would be done by the black worker, while the white worker would work mainly with white residents, although both workers would attend meetings of the two associations.

The worker felt that one driving force behind the Asian project was provided by the desire for mother tongue teaching and the need for a nursery. These did not in themselves have direct reference to housing issues; however the worker felt that the skills learnt in running a management committee could later be transferred to other areas. Indeed, the Asian project itself was to create interest groups such as an unemployment group and a women's group. However, in fact housing issues did not ever get on to the agenda of the Asian association. There may have been several reasons for this, among them the worker's reluctance to take up directly confrontational issues at the time.

Despite the divisions noted earlier between Mirpuris and Punjabis, both communities were represented on the committee. Meetings were unstructured and were held on a Sunday, the traditional free time for the community. Discussions were held about common political and often long-term issues such as mother tongue teaching. Often the group became impatient with an approach which stressed contact and pressure over an issue from the 'bottom up' rather than writing straight to the local MP, and the worker felt that it was his role in early

1982 to find an issue which was relevant and to keep motivation going in the following way:

I see my role with the group is to act as a motivator, to maintain the group's incentive, a resource agent to provide the group with information or referring them to sources where they can seek it for themselves, a facilitator, helping them interpret problems, and overall I try to offer support and help to maintain the cohesion of the group. Besides establishing my 'usefulness' to the group, I find it very important to gain the 'trust' of the groups in proving my neutrality. Finally, I try to recognise the sources of power within a group to mobilise it for the group's development, and to follow on, any intervention is guided by a knowledge of the social-economic positions of the chief activists.

Once meetings were formalised, and a constitution for the Sparth Asian Association was drawn up, the worker was able to withdraw from what had been a prominent and directive role. This was assisted by an MSC scheme which was run between 1982 and 1984, and whose two full-time and two part-time workers took on the casework and advice work function which the worker had filled. The SAA was also successful in finding a site for the teaching of Urdu; after much perseverance they persuaded the chief education officer to allow use of a local primary school on three evenings a week free of charge.

This experience of organisation as a pressure group meant that Asian residents were able to contribute significantly to the fight for a community centre for Sparthbottoms. Early in 1982 the residents' association approached the planning and estates department, on behalf of itself and the SAA, with the proposal that certain 'facelift' money (which paid for brick cleaning of housing) be used to build a community centre, an idea which had been put forward in the late 1970s. The council needed to be convinced that there was indeed a case for a centre, and it took a considerable amount of campaigning before the local authority was persuaded by their case.

In the event the community centre was funded by RMBC through inner areas funding, and once the centre was opened in 1985, educational and self-help activities were transferred there. Indeed Asian community activities were so strong that they dominated the activities of the centre, and although it was written into the constitution that there should be a balance of black and white members on the centre's management committee, Asian groups in fact came to form the majority. The Sparth Asian Association continued to be well attended and its focus of attention shifted to general issues such as long-term unemployment and health. The association was very much more confident, articulate and critical than it had been, something the white residents had been forced to adjust to. It was now normal for public meetings in Sparthbottoms, for example those with local authority officials, to be bilingual, with pauses for translation accepted as a matter of course.

Wardleworth

Wardleworth lies just to the north-east of Rochdale town centre and its boundaries include the River Roch to the south. Although a few large houses were built during the early part of the nineteenth century, the area was mainly developed as a residential area in the late nineteenth and early twentieth centuries. Many residents moved away following the loss of jobs after Beeching railway closures in the early 1960s, and immigrants from Pakistan and Bangladesh moved into the area. In 1981 Wardleworth had the highest levels of unemployment, almost double the borough average.

Parts of Wardleworth showed similar characteristics to that of Sparthbottoms with an elderly white and a young Asian population. A high proportion of housing was owner-occupied, with Asian homes showing the severest lack of basic amenities. Wardleworth CBAA was identified as the highest priority area; the first housing action area (HAA) was declared in 1976. By the early 1970s some residents had formed an improvement committee which resulted in some clearance and landscaping. The residents' association, serviced by officers from the CBAA team, campaigned on a variety of environmental issues such as clearance of derelict sites, the condition of roads and footpaths, and the nuisance caused by local industry. In 1980 the residents' association changed its name to the Wardleworth Community Association without any perceptible change of role.

Although community work in a general sense had been undertaken in Wardleworth for a number of years under the umbrella of the CBAA programme, when RCP workers started in April 1981, there was little input, other than some involvement in social activities by the area improvement team and the activities of the community centre. The centre, well used by the local Asian community, had been open for less than a year and was administered by the planning department. It appeared that the community centre was regarded predominantly as a service provided by the local authority which was fulfilling local needs through the paid worker, the centre warden; when questioned, residents felt no responsibility for its organisation or its management.

In order to support the warden of Wardleworth Community Centre in her objective of achieving an independent management structure, a user group was established which would gain experience of a centre management role and assist the warden in the provision of service. However, the two RCP workers found that a back-seat role did not allow serious community development to take place with the group, given what they perceived as a dependency on the warden. At that time CBAA officers were taking initiatives in relation to the funding of an extension to the centre. RCP workers saw in this another example of the council's directive approach which they considered detrimental to the development of self-determination and which went counter to the user group's developing management abilities. Following considerable conflict with the CBAA project leader, the workers decided to withdraw from that area of work.

Instead the workers turned fully towards the white community association, to which they had already begun to give attention. Here they saw the close co-operation with local authority officers and a consensus approach as a hindrance to its development, preventing it from obtaining an influential role in the area. Campaigns had usually been conducted by means of correspondence between the secretary of the association and various local authority departments. The relationship was further cemented, they believed, with the election of the community centre warden, an employee of the planning department, as secretary of the association. RCP workers worked with officers of the association to see how meetings could be made more effective. Gradually more people became actively involved and greater communication was opened up between the association and people in the area.

There are undoubtedly different interpretations and memories of RCP involvement in the residents association during those years. One of the workers says that 'my memory of this was feeling that we spent far too long trying to carry white residents with us', but the centre warden feels that the

RCP was unable to work with the white community association, effectively 'writing them off'. Moreover she feels that RCP did not prioritise residents' needs; while the association members were fighting for a larger kitchen for the centre, vital for its use for weddings and celebrations, RCP wanted a political debate. RCP, she says, were requiring groups to be self-activating from an early stage, while she saw a need for time to draw out skills while she 'worked from behind'.

Whatever the case, within the Asian community there was little understanding at the time of how the local authority worked. The black worker in this case felt that he should not immediately help Asian groups form around housing or environmental issues; they ran the risk of failure through lack of confidence and awareness which might prove counter-productive. What he did was slowly to introduce to some of the existing Asian groups and to groups he helped to form, experiences and formal skills which could be useful in their future negotiation with the local authority. Still within a familiar group context, many local Asians came into contact with councillors and council officers.

One of the first main areas of work for the black worker was support for the Bangladesh Family Advice Centre committee in their attempt through MSC funding to provide a basic advice-giving function. About 1,500 Bangladeshis lived in Rochdale, some 1,200 living in Wardleworth. Describing themselves as Rochdale's 'lost community', they attributed this not merely to their village background and language barrier, but to the fact that they remained unacknowledged by the authorities and services. They identified the following factors as crucial to the community: 80–90 per cent of Bangladeshis in Rochdale did not speak English; recession in the textile industry had hit hard, 90 per cent of heads of households now being unemployed; health, education, and welfare were affected by isolation. Their invisibility was, as they said, almost total.

The scheme received MSC, then urban aid funding for five years. The main priority of what became the Bangladesh Community Project was a community health scheme, but self-help groups were also established for elderly and unemployed men. It was hoped to start an Asian women's co-operative, but this did not materialise. Advice was given mostly on housing improvement grants, and the project workers developed a liaison role with the housing, education and health services.

In supporting the Bangladesh Community Project's staff members, the RCP worker recognised that such work might not be regarded as central to the RCP's objectives, given the central focus on housing and environmental issues. His own view was that work had to start at a much earlier stage, encouraging people to see the value of working together even in small groups, to deal with common problems, and to develop the confidence to tackle them.

This emphasis on confronting aspects of white culture, practice and organisation was even more apparent with the work that was done with the Kashmir Youth Movement. The worker encouraged the members to adopt a committee structure and systematic accounting procedures and subsequently to apply for registration with the Youth and Community Service. The scheme was finally funded with £172,000 through Inner Areas Programme funding and was designed in terms of industrial, educational and recreational provision.

The project criteria also made specific reference to the generation gap. The decline of the textile industry had resulted in disproportionate unemployment among Asians in comparison to their white counterparts, leading to increasing inter-generational conflict. British Asian youth, it was argued, lacked the confidence in the older generation and in many cases felt that the community leaders neither understood nor respected their views. They needed to have an opportunity to develop confidence and skills which were denied them because of discrimination and disadvantage. The project would try to 'build bridges back into society' for young Asians who had been made to feel they were not part of it. They portrayed their situation in the following way:

Asian youth feel neglected, alienated, resentful at the lack of facilities for them. This coupled with parental pressure and restrictions is making their problems worse. They are a generation growing in social isolation uncared for by both minority and majority communities. The most affected group are Asian girls. At present there is no provision for them at all.[1]

What both the Bangladesh Community Project and the Kashmir Advice Project had unearthed was a large number of fresh problems related to house improvement grant work. Towards the end of 1982, working closely with one of the RCP's white community workers, the Asian worker brought together a number of residents who had become familiar and confident with group processes to form what became known as the housing group.

During the next six or seven months the group investigated the problems experienced by many families in the area during and after house improvements. The group's findings were brought together in a detailed report which formed the basis of negotiations with the local authority on a number of issues. Members of the housing group, together with a number of other Asian residents, began to channel their interest through what had become a community association more able to represent the majority view on a variety of issues. Within two years a new style of organisation had emerged in Wardleworth which challenged the old hierarchies within the Asian community. A new generation had demonstrated an ability to negotiate and manage quite sizeable resources. Inevitably it introduced a new element into community life.

Milkstone

The second black member of the RCP team, an experienced council community worker, started work in the Milkstone area of Rochdale in late 1981. The Asian residents in Milkstone, unlike those in Sparthbottoms and Wardleworth, originated from an urban area in Pakistan, and – according to the analysis of the worker – were more likely to take risks than those from rural areas, setting up businesses and looking for educational opportunities for their children. There was also a significant number of families who came from East Africa and other countries. Many members of both the Pakistani population and these latter groups had business backgrounds and consequently their organisation and outlook on life was very different from the Asian community in Wardleworth.

Despite this there was a very poor take-up of improvement grants in the area. Not only was there a low level of activity around housing issues but the residents had no confidence in and little contact with the local authority. The worker therefore perceived his first task as making the council officers more receptive, sensitive and friendly. Over a six-month period informal meetings were held between the worker, local residents, the CBAA office staff and environmental health officers, meetings which over time began to take decisions.

At the same time the worker helped to establish a steering

group which arranged a public meeting early in 1982, at which a residents' association, representing the various ethnic groups in the area, was launched. This was a response in part to pleas from the council for a residents' group to whom both officers and councillors might relate, and in part to the need for a more representative local organisation than the street traders group. The move also met the needs of a previous Labour ward councillor, who was looking to renew his power base in the area. He became the first chairman of the association. In so doing, party politics became more firmly written into the fabric of community activity, his involvement causing outspoken opposition from the Liberals, including from the local MP.

With the community worker's support the association formed three sub-committees, two of which concentrated upon housing and environmental issues and held numerous meetings with council officials. The residents' association also sponsored an MSC-funded advice project and employed three Asian advice workers. During 1982 and 1983 the residents' association, the bulk of whose members had no previous experience of negotiating with the local authority, developed in such a way that its influence was felt across Rochdale as it started representing to the local authority views on more general issues such as education.

The association did not always achieve its demands, but the principle of negotiation and consultation was firmly established. On one occasion the residents' association insisted that houses which were to be sold to St Vincent's Housing Association were required for owner occupation, forcing a year-long consultation process to take place. Another enquiry was instituted when the residents challenged the demolition of 250 properties under compulsory purchase order (CPO). Although unsuccessful, a strong case was made to the housing department that Milkstone residents who were affected by compulsory purchase orders should be given high priority when the allocation of miscellaneous properties in Milkstone was decided. The principle was agreed to by the council, but not always followed through, causing frustration to residents.

Several blocks of housing in the area were 'enveloped' during the period. This involved the complete renewal of the outer skin, including walls, roof, windows and doors, and a sub-committee of the residents' association, the 'enveloping sub-committee', was particularly active in 1984/85, in some instances gaining grant allocations and in another instance obtaining compensation for damage to properties sustained while contractors were renovating them.

Council officers might reluctantly admit that the residents' association was able to do more 'lobbying, pushing and shoving than would have been done otherwise', but are reluctant to concede more impact on the council than to force consultation and a more open process. The RCP worker would agree with this, but would express it in a different way: 'Lobbying was there, but often residents were banging their heads against a brick wall.' Indeed, the loss of the right of sale of the Twedale Street houses, what appeared to be the insubstantial nature of the concessions on CPOs, the nervousness, indeed often negative reaction by officers to residents' criticisms during 'enveloping' negotiations, all called into question the real nature of the consultation. To what extent could this be seen as resident participation or manipulation in urban renewal?

However, it was the first time that a predominantly black group had begun to liaise directly with the local authority on CBAA related matters, and the press coverage received by the association left no one in any doubt about the impact made by the group. Council officers were willing at least to come to meetings and this had an effect not only on the Asian community but on the white community elsewhere in Rochdale, where more people felt able to argue the case with local officers on an individual basis. Furthermore, the grant take-up during this period appeared to increase among Asian householders and it might be argued that this related to the new-found confidence among the Asian community.

RCP workers and other observers would see that the effect of this pressure was that there was a general improvement in the way in which grants were administered in the borough. This would be strongly contested by the environmental health department, who see improvements as being due to increased staff levels, improved publicity and other levels of information, and contested the claims at the time. Yet to some extent there is a recognition that the council were forced to reassess what was an appropriate service; there was a realisation by some officers, for example, that the classification of kitchen extensions as a luxury was discriminatory in the context of the larger Asian family, where the kitchen was often the main room for the women.

However, whether this was real power needs to be explored further. The worker involved in the Milkstone enveloping feels that despite apparent successes by residents, serious mistakes were made by the council, insufficient money was granted to do internal work at the same time as external, many families being unable to return to their homes; ultimately he feels residents were dependent on council good will. Furthermore, as RMBC recognised, these areas remained the poorest and perhaps the most deprived of the borough, although both physically and socially the programme had been a success. Given the increasing unemployment rates throughout the inner areas, there were serious doubts about the level of future maintenance, or the contribution owners could continue to make to the improvement process. It was difficult to feel confident about the 'regeneration' of the areas under the circumstances. Furthermore, the very success of residents' groups could undercut their access to real power. Although street-level consultation continued for further schemes, it was a real possibility that over time new forms of consultation could even serve to undermine local residents' organisations and restrict the number of residents involved and consulted. If it was individual representatives on area committees who received the relevant papers, decisions could be seen to be made at that level; indeed some groups felt that they were no longer necessary in the context of area committees. Both CBAA teams and the community workers were aware of the need to ensure open access to area committees and to encourage their constituent organisations.

Yet these committees did reflect a powerful measure of information giving which was able to shape council perspectives, and to that extent reflect a maturing of attitude by the council. The varied nature of the representation on each area committee also represents the particular type of grassroots organisation in each area. RCP regarded area committees as important in the development of more formal structures of participatory democracy in Rochdale, particularly as they emerged from and explored issues of environmental and housing improvement which were of immediate material concern to people.

At the same time, when reviewing the functioning of the area committees, RCP had recognised some of the problem areas. Its workers had argued strongly for translation breaks at meetings and that papers to be translated into Urdu and Bengali where necessary. There was also clear concern about how decisions were being reached. An RCP discussion paper explained:

On issue of content reports tend to be designed for producing decisions rather than encouraging discussion. They put forward a limited number of options, giving all the factors leading towards those options in great detail, and conclude with clear-cut recommendations. This makes it difficult for others who have not been involved in the thinking behind a report to contribute to the decision. If officers were encouraged to prepare only the bare outline of an issue which needed to be considered this could leave more room for fresh thought.

In some areas the creation of area committees has stimulated activity, but in others RCP would recognise that they have detracted from the independence of residents' groups. One evidence of this is the extent to which representatives work to the agenda of the local authority rather than putting forward locally determined issues as agenda items. The danger is that the effort that might go into the smaller groups becomes dissipated as people get drawn into the area committees. Area committees can operate at several levels simultaneously: they may be drawing in representation at the level of a street, one block, a luncheon club. At the same time they operate as an open forum, theoretically encouraging free participation. It is indeed a reflection of their community-based nature that each committee is so distinctly different, responding to the realities in each locality.

And so the questions for the agency in such developments must remain how far the formalisation of communication with individuals might militate ultimately to weaken the power of the groups and lead to the formation of new élites, how far the council might be operating a more sophisticated level of paternalism, and to what extent the residents can acquire, through the area committees, merely an illusion of, or the actual power of decision making, an essential ingredient of social change.

4 Roles and Rules: Access to the Community

Alan Barr (1980), based on his experience at Oldham Community Project, offered the following advice on entry to the Asian community.

- Recognise national, regional and other geographical differences of origin.
- Work with younger people because there will be fewer problems about language, education and sex roles; for similar reasons work with people with an urban not a rural background.
- The worker may have to work with élites, that is those with enough worldliness and sophistication to be comfortable with people from other ethnic groups.
- Foster cultural identification with agents of change through ethnic workers or co-workers, translation, use of social networks and so on.
- Organise Asians through offering an individual advice and information service.
- Find a common self-interest across ethnic groups by:
  (1) detailed community analysis
  (2) looking at the needs of each ethnic group, and helping them to solve these first through an ethnic group approach
  (3) an education process that involves working frankly on internal divisions and stereotypes, and looking at the effects of immigration and causes of poverty outside the neighbourhood.

Even setting aside its stereotypical approach to Asian communities and the obvious dangers of such a proscriptive and prescriptive model, this analysis fails, despite its acknowledgement of regional and national differences, to recognise the diversity of social patterns within black communities, both on a macro and

47

micro level, conditioned not only by locality of origin, but by the varied impact of British urban society. In Rochdale the workers found that there were important economical and political networks and links which existed at a town-wide level. At the same time, locally, social and cultural life was often community-based and highly varied.

Alan Barr predicates trust, rather than the worker's value as a resource, as the most important factor. Most of the workers in this study, both black and white, however much they would emphasise the importance of trust, very often had to work in its very absence. But then the model offered is also a non-conflict one, which does not recognise a possible shift in the balance of power within the communities to non-élites. In the areas covered by this study younger people were not always easily accessible to the community worker. Where it was possible to work with younger people an approach was often required which meant opening up the control held by the older generation, usually involving working with both groups simultaneously. Even then the inter-generational conflict was sometimes a violent one.

An agency or community work approach which seeks to shift the balance of power within the community might find that working with those from an urban background often excluded the possibility of working not only with the largest group but the working class, and poorest sections of the black community. Alan Barr's analysis questions the very object or purpose of the intervention itself. Also absent is the worker's own political and community development perspective in its agency setting. The worker's style is often directed by his or her own experience and identity, and initial relationship with the community, as well as by the constraints of the agency and particular characteristics of the neighbourhood. Nowhere is this more in evidence than at the point of access to the community.

Furthermore, the community leader is sometimes a moving target. The identification of a leader by the local authority and the community itself frequently diverges. In some areas of our study we find that local authority officers were forced to accept a more diversified leadership, but it remained true that the person who made the loudest noise and to whom the local authority looked was not necessarily the one responding to and trusted by the community.

Workers and leaders

The struggle which engaged the Al-Hilal community worker in Cheetham Hill from 1981 arose from the reorganisation of secondary education in Manchester, which had the effect of excluding Muslim teenage girls in Cheetham Hill from the nearest single sex school. Parents were faced with the choice of accepting the neighbourhood coeducational school or of sending the girls across the city centre to a single sex school in the south of the city. A number of parents of Muslim girls refused to send their daughters to either of these schools and went on school attendance strike.

For the community worker, as a Muslim parent, the struggle was also his own. The action related too closely to a considered threat to his own beliefs and culture for him to remain either neutral or to prioritise the process over the outcome. The active campaign that was fought was the first time that the community had confronted the local authority collectively. Yet this collective action was limited; there were many times when the worker felt unable to bring along with him the group of parents with whom he closely worked, let alone hand responsibility to them, for fear that their lack of confidence and inexperience in dealing with local authority officers would prejudice the outcome. Public demonstration, even more than private meetings, witnessed the community worker as leader, heading the demonstration to the town hall, interviewed by the media. 'It was in those times,' the worker recalls, 'that the inner Pakistani me, that Muslim person used to take over from the community worker.'

The longer he worked with the issues and was involved in decision making, the more his leadership role was strengthened, reinforced by council officers' perception of him. For the council, without access to a wide group of people, the apparent reasonableness and articulacy of someone who was claiming to represent major parts of the community was irresistible. On the other hand, a group of parents associated with the campaign were also developing views and perspectives which were not necessarily those of the worker. For many years previously active informally in community affairs, he had been aware that there would be a painful transition from community activist to paid worker accountable to some of the people he had helped to develop initially. Sometimes, however, he lost sight of the fact that he did not have the right to speak on behalf of everyone. To that extent the community work and leadership function sat uneasily together.

It has been argued that there are reasons for community workers to play a dominant role in meetings with white council officers or members, where Asian group members may experience themselves in a subordinate role. The example of a black community worker is one way of showing that it is possible to confront officials without leading, as a rule, to ill feelings and withdrawal of officers and members from such discussions. In that situation the worker might simultaneously need to make it clear that she is not seeking power on her own behalf. However there is a real danger of confusing the group if the worker is trying to build the self-confidence and cohesion of its members in the long term as well as being misunderstood by those community work observers who are accustomed to a non-directive style. The principle community development officer in Manchester comments;

One of the crucial areas of conflict in regard to the role of the worker was that the traditional model places emphasis on the democratic process. The non-directive approach is never one achieved completely by the worker, but it is important that the worker does not take on a major role. In terms of internal group dynamics, it is not necessary to get approval of the whole group, but on the other hand, the worker should not get caught up in doing a lot for the group and speaking for it.

In Cleveland the first neighbourhood worker for ethnic minorities worked from a similar relationship and high status position in relation to the community, encouraging the social services department to adopt an approach which identified, and worked with 'key figures' within the community. By contrast, the perception of the third worker, appointed in 1984, was that as a woman and from an Indian background, she was distanced from the male leadership within the majority Pakistani community. Moreover her own neighbourhood work perspective was at odds with the priority of the community leaders – to obtain resources for community centres. Her view was that channelling funds into the community through a small number of dominant male figures was incompatible with community development. Certainly it did not promote what was crystallising as the fundamental objective of neighbourhood work in Cleveland: the promotion of more jobs and services, and a

challenge to racism within the structure of the service providers, above all the local authority.

This example, while important within the local context, is
not put forward to make any general statement; indeed generalisations would be misleading if not dangerous. Another Indian
woman, working with the Asian Youth Project in Cheetham,
also felt at a disadvantage in terms of her perceived status by
the male Pakistani leadership. On the other hand, in South
Manchester, working in Moss Side, another worker found that
neither her status as a woman nor her position as an Indian was
an issue when working with the Pakistani community. Her view
is that effective work can be done if it is based on the community need, and is carried on in a low-key, non-confrontational
way; most criticism will die down and tensions can be avoided.
She and other women in Manchester, she believes, have been
able to develop styles of work which have bypassed the community 'leaders' altogether. This view is not altogether
accepted by all the workers in this study. Some feel that so long
as certain individuals are excluded from power and decision
making within the community, it may not be possible or even
desirable to avoid confrontation, if community development is
to have an educational role. Moreover in Cleveland, for
example, the workers felt that community leaders' expression
of needs encompassed a desire to control which was not seen
as legitimate.

Yet the Cleveland neighbourhood worker had recognised that
it would not be possible to bypass the community leaders
altogether. Indeed it would be necessary to obtain their confidence in order to retain a credible liaison, support and resource function within the black community. She opted to gain
that confidence through raising awareness of rights and inequalities in service provision.

This dilemma was also evident in Rochdale. There were
obvious benefits in working with individuals in the community
who had political leverage and access to power; indeed in some
cases it did not seem wise to ignore the existing networks of
influence. Both black workers in RCP had links with the mosque
in their respective areas, although mosque politics were the
most volatile of all.

Yet the workers in all the areas agree that, whatever the
tactics pursued, reinforcing leadership patterns and developing
communities were antithetical. In Rochdale a decision was

taken early on to work as far as possible at a very local level, with streets and blocks of houses rather than with whole areas. This in itself was breaking the mould of local authority thinking, which had traditionally worked with large residents' associations or with one or two powerful individuals. The street approach threw up a more complex network of smaller organisations within communities. Although the 'block scheme' model was not a feature to the same extent in Wardleworth and Sparthbottoms, parallel tactics of small group organisation were used and had similar repercussions. This had implications in terms of the amount of worker time and local authority resources needed to respond on a very local level.

The worker assigned to Wardleworth and Sparthbottoms, a Bangladeshi, came from outside the majority Pakistani community, without family or social links. With no obvious position in the hierarchy, he was at an obvious advantage in developing a stand which was to an extent independent of power bases.

In both Wardleworth and Sparthbottoms the worker aimed to demonstrate the effectiveness of pressure group activities. This meant breaking with the traditional practice, transferred from Pakistan, of individuals or families approaching problems in an isolated way and trying to solve them through personal contact or direct access to those understood to have more power, such as the local MP, rather than the relevant department of RMBC. The worker's approach was wholly compatible with his decision to bypass the town's mosques and Pakistan welfare associations, whom residents had always been inclined to turn to for assistance with personal problems in the past.

Paradoxically the perceived need to gain initial trust forced the worker into two apparently contradictory positions. The first was that he became involved in individual casework mainly related to home improvement grants. It was this aspect of his strategy which caused most conflict with his white colleagues, who considered that a 'Mr Fix-it' role lay somewhere between that of social worker and community leader, and as such was incompatible with a community development input.

The second was that it became necessary on occasions to work with key figures while establishing the organisational focus which would allow a challenge to middle class leadership to take place. Access to the Bangladeshi community was through the chairman of the Bangladesh Association, a consultant physician from outside the area, who was interested in obtaining MSC project funding. It was through his support that the worker was able to make contact among unemployed textile workers and it was this group which within a few years altered the nature of community activity and group leadership within the Bangladeshi community. There was an element among the leadership within the community which initially explored the possibilities of functioning from within the Wardleworth Community Association. Unable to see its value, within a short time it was left open for the younger element from the Kashmir Youth Project and the Bangladesh Community Project. Eventually it became possible for people who had no established links within the community to take up positions within the community association, and for those community activities to provide the stepping stone to seats on school governing bodies and the council's consultative committees.

Issue-based work
The white co-worker in Wardleworth in 1981–83 was newly trained and had no experience of working with Asian communities. A lot of his early time, he reflected was spent 'stumbling into things rather than making a lot of sense of things'. Writing in January 1982 he described his dilemma: 'What little I know about working with Asian people seems to come in the form of negative strictures. I have very little positive information to work on, with which to begin answering questions for myself.' It was almost inevitable then that he should feel his position to be peripheral to the main thrust of developments in the area.

One unsatisfactory option existed: to follow the work pursued by his black colleague without being able to properly fit together the pieces. Not that a strategy which embraced casework and key leadership was one which he could readily accept. It would probably take the confidence of experience and a willingness to analyse afresh based on an understanding of the local community to accept such a challenge to commonly understood principles. It was only as casework began to soak up a lot of time and it became apparent that more global strategies were needed that the long-term picture began to emerge. Work began to crystallise more obviously around housing issues. As a strategy was needed for putting a case to the council about adequate information to residents on the grant system, and better building standards, he was able to define a role for himself.

It was at this point that some of the younger men, some of whom were involved with the Bangladesh and Kashmiri projects, had begun to recognise the need to take on issues on a broader basis. Taking up seats on the management committee of the Wardleworth Community Association and working with the purpose and experience derived from their groups, it was then that the value of the broader strategy became apparent.

Housing and environmental sub-groups were formed. Between 1981 and 1983 the white worker was able to build up a relationship with the younger men, and both workers worked with these groups, who started a dialogue with the council in the same way as the residents' associations elsewhere. In the summer of 1983 they printed a document critical of the administration of grants and supervision of building standards and presented it to the council.

The lack of access into Asian male public politics can evidently be experienced as a disadvantage by white male community workers. This is even more the case for women, whose status can exclude them altogether from certain kinds of group work. By the same token white women have found that their gender has been a positive attribute in their work with Asian women, a knowledge of inter- and intra-communal politics having less importance.

One of the women workers at RCP, working in 1984 in Deeplish, another inner city area in Rochdale made initial contact with the UK Islamic Mission following council moves to bring the mission and other groups together with the residents' association in an inner areas bid for a community centre. However, the Asian representatives on the residents' association, worried that the proposed centre would become another teaching centre, were antagonistic to the mission's involvement, and a public meeting was organised to protest such a development.

The worker found that it was difficult for her to place Asian leadership within a context, or even accurately to assess the influence of individuals within the area. In this situation selective contact was less than useful, and the worker, anyway more at ease with a 'grassroots' approach, felt that 'doorknocking' in the area was more productive.

In the worker's estimation, the Deeplish residents' association did later show itself to have gained a strong base in the Asian community, building credibility, she felt, through its neutral position in the community. Immediately after a public meeting concerning the community centre, there were 8 Asian representatives out of 12 on the committee. However, this was shortlived as the committee failed to survive a variety of internal problems.

The difficulty for the worker was that she was unable to identify with certainty the elements in her strategy which had been effective. Clearly bypassing sources of power and patronage through lack of information and choosing to do so with knowledge are not the same thing. It was crucial that the worker was unable to have any real sense of her own credibility and this had important effects on sustaining confidence in her work with Asian communities in the area, and made her vulnerable to criticism. Deeplish presented particularly complex political issues and in relation to the community centre members of the residents' association were putting forward preconditions which were quite unacceptable to the mosque. One of RCP's black workers had been working in the area for some time, and in such a situation it was particularly important that knowledge should be shared between team members. In fact, there were possibly too many of the team in the same locality without their work areas being sufficiently defined. Certainly there was an absence of shared purpose or discussion. The result was that 'anyway I felt that I had never been given a brief to work with the Asian community and always felt that I was tresspassing on the other worker's territory'.

In this situation there was considerable ambivalence by the black worker concerning his white colleague's involvement in the area. Black community workers may feel cynical, even angry at a perceived approach by white people which assumes that an anti-racist approach and a superficial understanding of black 'needs' gives them credibility. Given the imperial past and present racism, compounded with language barriers, some argue, there would always be an unequal situation, particularly when working with the older generation. Community work is about getting to know people, and to the extent that a community feels that it does not 'know' the worker, it can be argued, it may also be unable to criticise which is an essential part of the working relationship.

On the other hand many white workers feel no such credibility, finding an approach to racism which often derived from theoretical debate inadequate in the face of blatant street level racism. Given the need first to conquer their own apprehension in going into communities of which they knew little, it would be unrealistic to expect a ready response to their own racism or to that encountered in the neighbourhoods. A failure to respond as a team to such difficulties can lead to a situation where white workers feel disabled in a multi-racial locality, despite a real desire to identify and build strategies to counter racism, both internal and external to the agency.

It is in this area of motives and interpretation that understanding between team members, particularly black and white, needs to be clarified. Division of work because of practical considerations such as language skills and the advantage of ethnic and cultural identity may lead to suspicion among black workers that their white colleagues are not taking on responsibility for working with black people. At the same time they may feel considerable ambivalance about white colleagues' involvement with black groups, particularly if there has been no discussion on different styles or objectives. White workers for their part may perceive real or imagined cues about trespassing on black workers 'territory'. The only way forward involves open discussion within teams and between co-workers.

Working with women

In Middlesbrough the two neighbourhood workers found that their attempts to work effectively with women were frustrated in several ways. The operation of hierarchies, the existence of street and institutional racism, the inappropriate nature of community work solutions for Asian women in the area, all served to call into question the medium of self-help groups. Their expectations of work with women had derived from a general view that Asian women were isolated and that there were concerns around health care, health education, and dietary provision. They were also aware of the need to approach the issue of domestic violence. However, it became apparent that in the context of Central Middlesbrough any sort of counselling organisation would have to be established under the patronage of male leaders. This would not have provided the safe environment required for the young women, nor did it sit easily with ideas which the workers held about women's development. They very quickly realised that it would be wrong to assume that issues important to white women would necessarily be ones which black women felt able to tackle. Often the issues existed, but at the point of taking collection action, there was no response from the women themselves.

The workers contacted Asian professional women in appropriate services in the community with a view to offering support to existing groups. What they found was that the power structures among the men were duplicated among professional black women and there was a resistance to moves which might threaten their position.

An Asian young girls' class had been set up by Middlesbrough Borough Council with great difficulty, as the concepts of groups for other than cultural and religious purposes at that time in the early 1980s was an alien one. Even such a group with quite limited goals could be seen as threatening to the extent that it provided opportunity for discussion. An Asian women's sewing class came under pressure when the women attending were harrassed in the street. The conclusion drawn by the workers was not only that support and contact with women had to continue through agencies, but work with women on an individual basis was also a valid activity in terms of community development. A woman who left home or went into a refuge was challenging the norm in a very real sense, and required personal support in the absence of group structures.

When another black woman worker joined the Cleveland Neighbourhood Work team in 1986 she found the Asian girls' group still in existence, run by the community centre manager and white women volunteers. Attendance had been poor, but at the beginning of 1987 the group re-formed with older girls and she and a male colleague were invited by the girls to discuss how they could be self-managing. The girls felt that they needed skills in such areas as group dynamics, and wanted to know about committees and funding. Both workers were keen to contradict the stereotype of Asian girls, and felt that there was no reason why a man should not work with Asian women, given a sensitive but not overly-cautious approach. As with white workers in the context of black groups, the male worker feels, men can create problems in working with Asian women and girls through their own lack of confidence. The issue of male involvement can become more sensitive than it need be as a result of an individual's own attitudes and fear of going beyond an imaginary line: 'What is sensitive is people's own perceptions.' When the group had originally formed it had been agreed that there would be no male involvement, but things had changed since then. Having said that, the second worker adds that it remained true that they were not interested in collective action. 'What they want to do is to get together and talk; they are not an issue-taking community.'

By contrast the worker points out a Muslim Women's Group in Stockton-on-Tees, which met in a local community centre, was largely very successful and 'all issues are up for discussion'. Although there are three professional working women on the management committee, in the main the group is comprised of non-working women from rural backgrounds. The worker's view is that the women in the community in Stockton appear to be less restricted and open to new ideas, able to get out at weekends and in the evenings.

There also seemed to be a possibility of the development of self-help groups in North Thornaby, situated just to the south-east of Stockton, where there had been little previous community work. The worker found a number of single parents, whose husbands had left them, whose absence of self-identification as single parents closed them off from support systems. The first steps seemed to be to bring individuals together, building slowly and carefully from that basic contact.

What became apparent to the Middlesbrough workers was that in order to understand and develop their work with women in a meaningful way, it would be necessary to understand in greater detail factors which had to do not just with culture but with patterns of immigration which would help to explain the differences between communities. This was a view shared by one of the workers in Rochdale who found that the use of a similar approach in different areas could produce different results. Working in Deeplish she had found it impossible to gain access to women, while in Newbold her experience was quite different for reasons she was unable to explain. Several enthusiastic and powerful black women had attended initial meetings held by the council to explain the operation of community-based areas. Later, able to 'doorknock' together with both local white and black women, a real interest by women residents was revealed, many of whom were homeworkers.

The experience of working with women in Manchester has been quite different, and in itself varied. In Cheetham where the women's discussion groups led by the Al-Hilal Community Project's youth worker centred mainly around Islamic beliefs and customs, there was a perceived change from the early days of

the project. Outreach workers had encouraged women previously reluctant to come out of the home. An Asian women's
health group, held for eight weeks in 1987, had attracted very
good attendance, and particularly of older women, who had not
previously joined other activities.

In south Manchester one worker's experience dates back to
the early 1970s when as a Punjabi-speaking Indian Hindu she
first started working with the Muslim Pakistani community in
Moss Side. The profile of the Pakistani population was changing
as single men were joined by their families. Starting work in the
Moss Side Community Project, an advisory centre funded by
the Mothers' Union and the British Council of Churches, she
found that rising unemployment was throwing up a whole range
of issues including homelessness. There were also issues relating specifically to women, including cases of domestic violence.
The worker decided to work only with women and children, not
introducing herself to the male leaders or within the mosque. In
many ways she would learn effective ways of working with
women through trial and error, but she was clear that the
advantage of a low profile was that she was not involved in
conflicts with doctrinaire religious leaders that could have
sapped her energy. 'I did have a political perspective, but I did
not want to be led into confrontation with the male leadership
which was becoming aware of its own power structure within a
new emerging society.'

At the time there were a few isolated community workers
working with the Asian community in South Manchester, often
without the necessary support from their management committees or from each other. In 1975 the worker became involved in the development of the Asian Youth and Community
Workers' Association which was set up initially as a self-help
group, and turned its attention to the needs of younger women.
The schools system was not offering Asian girls identity and
self-esteem, and she felt that concepts such as 'cultural conflict'
and 'generation gap' were oversimplifying the more complex
issues. A young people's centre, the Tippu Sultan Centre, with
MSC funding for four workers, set up a counselling service
based at one of the girls' schools. The worker also became
involved with the Sikh community, who had largely arrived in
Manchester in the late 1940s and for whom the issue of racism
within schools was a major issue.

The Asian Youth and Community Workers' Association itself

became the location of a dispute between those with a low-profile approach to community work, and those whose emphasis was overtly political. One male committee member formed the Pakistani Workers' Association, which had political aims and had no links with community work, while some of the women began to focus on issues such as immigration. Funding for the Tippu Sultan Centre was not renewed and the women's refuge also became a focus for conflict between the two groups, those women who had been involved in its early development resigning. The view of the worker was that the second group was interested in forming a political lobby about Pakistanis in Manchester rather than having a grounding in community development or being interested in provision. The group associated with the women's refuge became a focus for benefits, anti-deportation and other activity.

Such a political lobby itself, she feels, was essential, but the interests of both sides would have been better separated out earlier, rather than setting up to the two approaches in opposition to each other. Another community worker in the area points out that, at the practical level, involvement in issues such as housing, harrassment and deportation implied a major time commitment. That, and the high media profile which seemed inevitably to accompany any campaigning activity, put at risk the work possible at a grass-roots level. Neither, she feels, could such activity take with it at that stage the women she was supporting, who were beginning to organise into sewing or keep fit classes: 'The two groups just don't cross paths.'

The question raised then is not whether direct political engagement is necessary, but whether a worker can continue to be effective as a community development worker once personally identified in a front-line political role, as opposed to maintaining a motivating, but less directive political perspective. Yet, at a time when communities are under severe economic pressure, when access to resources through group activities attains an illusory quality, to some the very concept of comunity development may seem called into question, the need to apply more direct pressure more immediate.

In the period following the dissensions in the Asian Youth and Community Workers' Association, the worker moved away from a direct community development role and in 1982 was appointed to the post of district co-ordinator for community education, working with broad mainstream provision through

the local authority, concentrating on provision of basic education for Muslim women. She is now developing training courses
for women. A pilot course recruited 19 women between the
ages of 19 and 40, largely Muslim, entirely from the voluntary
sector, and with little formal education, who wanted to do some
community work. The course was designed to explore their
functioning as a group. Entitled 'Skills in working with Asian
communities', it was structured on needs expressed by
participants and included issues such as the local authority
structure, how to get funding, acceptable committee
structures, community worker roles, working with younger
women, and issues to do with sexuality and gender. Following
the course, the women wanted to meet on a monthly basis to
explore issues in greater depth, such as concepts of team work
and processes of group consultation and how differently such
concepts work in different cultural settings.

This Manchester worker's conclusion about the value or
relevance of group work to Asian women differs from that of the
Middlesbrough team, and both would agree that it underlines
the need to avoid general assumptions about approach. The
Pakistani community in South Manchester had become more
integrated within British structures, and the new generation of
youth and neighbourhood workers derived partly from women
who had been educated in Britain, found no prospects in low-
paid employment, and who looked to voluntary work as an
alternative to full-time involvement in the home. An example of
this sort of development was a young girls' group established in
the early 1970s. It operated at the end of a school day in a single
sex school with the assistance of an enthusiastic teacher and
some of the mothers. Despite some setbacks in the early years,
there was fresh input from mothers, one of whom drove a
minibus, and the group began to flourish, looking for and managing their own funds. One of the women obtained initial
training and became paid as a qualified youth worker in a part-
time job at another centre. Youth clubs were not always seen as
suitable for young girls, but this group, taking girls between the
ages of 13 and 17, covered such areas as self-defence, horse-
riding, skating, jewelry-making, as well as the more traditional
areas of cookery and sewing.

In contrast to the perceptions in Middlesbrough, this worker
identifies a high level of political awareness in the women she
has worked with. Aware of their own life-styles in terms of their

own and their husbands' relative levels of freedom and access
to money, they are alert to racism, and to how their children
and they themselves are treated at schools and have strong
opinions about family planning and the health services.
Moreover, they have developed a knowledge of Pakistani
politics, and a strong awareness of class brought with them
from their own rural background, an analysis which is applied to
their own experiences in Britain of racial harassment and treat-
ment in social services and other offices. The priority lies in
channelling this awareness into pressure for change.

Community worker as mediator

Even where the community worker has worked effectively in a
neighbourhood for several years, case studies have shown that
later developments, such as factional conflict, may prevent the
continuation of effective community work. The reason for this is
the difficulty the worker has in avoiding identification with one
group or the other. Attempts to re-emphasise neutrality
through mediation may be one way to re-engage in effective
work.

One community worker describes his work in the Cheetham
Hill area of Manchester in the late 1970s, the same area in
which the Al-Hilal project was located in the 1980s. The
background was the loss of various facilities to the local community as a result of redevelopment and their replacement by a
new multi-purpose centre on the edge of the area, set up by the
council. As a result of the reaction by a number of groups and
individuals that the centre was imposed on them, was inappropriate to community needs, and badly located, a number of
community groups came together with the aim of securing and
running a community centre which they could jointly manage,
and formed a community association. After a campaign of three
years, the basement of the former library was agreed upon and
converted for use as a centre. The advice centre was the first to
move there in 1977 and the Muslim group used the library for
Ramadan that autumn.

At the beginning of 1977 a major split occurred within the
Muslim group. Part of the dispute was over the use of the
mosque, religious interpretation and the failure to make progress in establishing a new Muslim centre and activities for
young people. One faction boycotted the election of Muslim
group officers and formed an independent group, the Madrassa.

The Madrassa then joined the association and used the library for its activities; it also participated fully in the running of the centre and association meetings. Conversely, the Muslim group, which had been one of the founder members, made only occasional use of the library, and took no active part in the association. Both the Muslim group and the Madrassa applied separately to use the library for Ramadan prayers in the summer 1978. It was not practicable to allow both groups in separately and neither would join in the prayers of the other. After lengthy discussion hosted by the association, no common ground was found. The association was left with the option of turning down both applications or granting one group exclusive use. A decision was formally made in favour of the Madrassa, largely on the grounds of their closer, though shorter involvement in, and support of the community association. The decision led to the resignation of the Muslim group and to heightened tension in the area.

Not only had the community association achieved very limited success at that time in its attempts to promote understanding between groups in the area, but the effectiveness of the community worker as a link person seemed to be placed in question. He had tried to remain neutral in the formal and informal discussions which had taken place, attempting to clarify the options open to the factions concerned, and to the community association's executive committee, and to arbitrate when requested. However, in practice it was almost impossible to retain or be seen to hold a neutral position when conflicting demands arose. After the decision was made about use during Ramadan, the worker lost any trust he had built up with the Muslim group because of his continuing involvement with the association.

After March 1980 the community work post was held by an experienced black worker who concentrated on building links with the Muslim group, encouraging members to pursue their own activities and make a grant application for funds for the development of their own centre. At the same time he helped the Madrassa draw up a constitution which allowed some involvement from the Muslim group. As an Afro-Caribbean and someone who had not been involved in the previous Ramadan dispute, he felt that it was possible for him to perform this mediating role from a neutral position outside the community. Nevertheless, there were times when the worker felt that he was seen as a spy by both sides, while his experience as a black person did not always seem valued by either group. Indeed as an employee of the social services department there were inherent difficulties in dissociating entirely from the previous decision, and to rebuild levels of trust.

However, the worker regarded it as important that in his role he should bring the two groups together to show unity over deeply felt issues, in building a new mosque, and he had some success in encouraging the two groups to co-operate with each other and with other black groups in a campaign to warn people of the likely effects of the 1981 British Nationality Act.

Another area where the worker was able viably to hold a mediating position was in working openly with young men who were often finding some of the constraints of family and religious life difficult. This echoes the work of the Birmingham Asian Resource Centre. Ranjit Sondhi indicates that the centre is often in the centre of controversy between those who favour continuity and those who desire change. It adopts the general principle that social development and reconstruction arise from a frank and open, as opposed to covert and apologetic discussion of both inter- and intra-group stresses and strains associated with Asian society. The belief is that as long as the social reorganisation of ethnic minority groups is founded on the ideals of an open society, what is valuable in tradition must survive and what ceases to be relevant in the present context be discarded. (Sondhi, 1982, p. 170)

It is essential that the community development worker take time to understand the local situation and avoid forming hasty alliances with particular sectional interests. It might be difficult to distinguish this from the 'value neutral' approach discussed by Harry Bragg and Nick Derricourt (1982). Yet there is an important distinction, even if at times it appears to be a difficult one to maintain. The worker cannot avoid making choices about which groups to work with in terms of resource redistribution, while at the same time avoiding being pulled into alliances at times of inter- or intra-group conflict. In Cleveland the neighbourhood work section's emphasis on neutrality was precisely to avoid alliances with specific groups at a time of internal conflict.

This attempt to stand outside inter-group conflict need not be confused with a mediatory role. It is often a hard task to get beyond perceptions of the worker as mediator both by the local authority and by the community. In some respects black workers appear to have to re-educate agencies, to fight again against the role placed on white community workers a decade ago. On the other hand, pressures for black workers may be greater, the role harder to dismiss; both agencies and communities ask black workers to translate for them not only in the literal sense, but to interpret whole cultures. The particular political and social organisation of the community and the political will and understanding of the agency will determine how possible it is for the worker to escape the pressures of these demands.

Pre-existing local conditions must influence the development of Asian communities. Commentators in Cleveland have characterised its society and local government structure and functioning as patriarchal and paternalistic. Service provision is highly centralised and the focus remains on that centralised provision rather on locally run services. Rochdale is a cotton town, 'built on the notion of deference', and highly politicised. In both, the concept of the leader in Pakistani rural and political life is reinforced by the political traditions of the local white community. It is not surprising to see community development interwoven with politics; the task for the worker is to show that there are other ways into the system other than through political patronage. While being sensitive and aware of existing patterns and determinants of leadership, the worker's approach should recognise that social reorganisation is both possible and present in Asian communities.

5 Towards a Team Perspective: The Worker within the Agency

The importance of design

For fear that we are turning away from the worker, at this stage our study returns to the worker within the agency, and examines the issues facing multi-racial teams working in a multi-racial society. Our starting point must be the design and objectives of any project. The important question is whether an agency acknowledges the presence of racism, both internal and external, when developing strategy and action, and can identify its manifestations and incorporate a challenge to that racism in its basic strategy. Project workers would draw attention to the fact that the understanding of race issues by both CPF nationally and politicians and officers of a town like Rochdale were very different in 1980/81 from the awareness gained by the latter part of the 1980s. Moreover, RCP's project director would add:

It must be recognised that for a national agency moving into a small town like Rochdale and establishing the hybrid which became RCP there were enormous difficulties. Including into the design an element which concentrated on confronting racism in a direct way might at that time have had the result of killing off the negotiations altogether.

However, placing our comments within an historical context may well help to evaluate how far lessons have been truly learnt or perceptions and actions altered over time.

There was then a fundamental flaw in the initial project design. At the very least individual workers would have to confront street-level racism, and both individuals and the agency itself would have to respond to institutional racism as exemplified in the services. In the case of RCP, the project's

66

reports and letters to the press would demonstrate that this was the case. Indeed, by 1985 the project was discussing moving from a rearguard position to a more aggressive stand as it considered working against racism on housing estates.

Yet RCP had been set up as a housing project with specific objectives which prioritised resident participation in urban renewal. Early pressure from CBAA staff for the project to move into 'softer' and less contentious areas of community development, such as play and social activities increased the team's determination to hold to the original objectives, and this is where the central focus lay. CPF nationally would argue that local considerations were the determining factors. On the other hand, RCP would argue that the team did not know how much room there was for manoeuvre, that 'reactions to early attempts to determine our boundaries indicated that we were CPF's *housing* project'. Although such a brief was not inherently inimical to an anti-racist approach, it gave rise to inflexible attitudes among some of the white team members about working methods. An open acknowledgement of the importance of racism as a determining factor in the life and development of communities might have promoted a more flexible concept of work appropriate in a multi-racial area, whether that work related to urban renewal or to any other issue.

The project started without two of its key workers. Moreover, as is frequently the case, not only was the project director unfamiliar with CPF, his parent agency, when he started, but he was unclear about the boundaries of the project: how far the funding constrained its action. Even had his analysis at this stage led him to widen the project's remit, there were more immediate concerns. Early days spent finding adequate accommodation, or resolving relationships within the team, meant that there was little time to question the fundamental purpose of the project or to consider its wider implications. It is the characteristic of many organisations that they become absorbed in how they survive within their environment without ever thinking through their basic purpose or recognising their own inherent contradictions.

CPF nationally would agree that there was no detailed development plan in the early stages. However, it was 'accepted that things were not going to be the same given the high levels of Asian population', and CPF recognised the need to consider the relative merits of multi-racial or separate ethnic organisation in the promotion of black people's interests. One worker would say 'that part of the problems specific to RCP, its design, its early history and its personalities, was that there was never a clear consensus that we should be working towards a strategy of any sort'. The fact that CPF worked to a high level of local autonomy militated to a large extent against some of these issues being thought through in detail at a national level. Given what should have been an interplay between Rochdale Community Projects locally and CPF nationally in determining objectives, this was not really a tenable position. Where national structures impinge on the local in recruitment processes, for example, a relative lack of inter-action can prevent local perceptions from being translated into change. Indeed, it is important that project members felt at a later stage that lessons learnt in Rochdale were not being effectively learnt by CPF centrally.

It was hoped that dual or joint working between black and white team members would be seen as a model of inter-ethnic relations which could be duplicated. However, the word 'racism' was not mentioned in the area profiles nor in the area objectives which were completed in the second half of 1981. Given that any real acknowledgment of racism as a base-line factor had been absent in the project design, a reference to racism at this point might well have set up a series of contradictions which it would have proved difficult to contain.

The first-line contradiction is that often even the equal opportunities dimension is absent from the structures of the agency. Interviews for posts are frequently set up by senior management, unfamiliar with either the neighbourhoods or their communities. Job descriptions make little reference to the requirements of work with black people, and personnel specifications – where they exist – are unable to grapple with the skills and experiences really required by the worker. Interview panels are often all white and dominated by men. It is not surprising in these circumstances to see that all successful candidates, sometimes all candidates, are white.

RCP was no exception to this model. At the time personnel specifications were not used in interviews, and there was no thought of choice of a selection panel which reflected an understanding of local black community issues. And it would be unrealistic in these circumstances to expect later appointments in the project's life to break the initial mould. Although, without success, a certain amount of effort was put into the recruitment of a black office-based worker, subsequent field-worker appointments never properly considered equal opportunities, let alone the experience of working with black groups, or of working with Asian women, or even language skills as priority criteria for appointment. Instead, reference was made back to the initial objective of the project – housing work.

This meant effectively that the only black workers in the project were those seconded by the council. There were many ramifications following from this. To the extent that none of the CPF employees had been recruited with specific reference to experience or skills relevant to working in multi-racial areas, and the black council employees were accredited precisely with those qualifications, this meant that from the start, despite the 'joint working' system, a very major burden of responsibility was being placed on the black workers for working with black people. In addition, the black workers might well have asked themselves whether RCP considered that RMBC had provided all that was necessary by way of black experience. The two black seconded workers were originally on section 11 funding which to a certain extent defined the areas in which they were working. Once this funding ceased and the workers' salaries were moved into the mainstream budget, there was more flexibility in terms of their working in white neighbourhoods.

The basic design of the project then, is crucial; early planning can also vitally affect the future development of the project. CPF had been invited to set up the project without consultation with existing workers in the area; the feelings after several years are that the secondment itself 'was more or less imposed upon us'. This is not an unusual situation and one from which lessons could be learnt. One of the workers had been working autonomously with the council, and consideration might well have been given to difficulties he might have in joining a team with precise and in many respects externally defined objectives. Moreover, when the project team first arrived in Rochdale in mid-1981, both black workers were away on a training course, joining the team only at the end of the year. This meant that all the initial profile work on the areas was done in their absence, although it was recognised by the white workers that they were unable to make an adequate assessment of black communities. They were unwilling to put in writing comments with which the black workers, already familiar with the neighbourhoods, would later disagree.

RCP would assert that the area objectives were not agreed until the black workers joined the project. At least one of the workers remembers it differently. All could agree that the major groundwork for decision making had already been covered and that the first week-long objective-setting session was tense, adversarial and set the scene for later disputes. For one of the black workers, a council worker with many years experience, the position seemed irreversible: his part in decision making, even his ability to identify who made decisions, were apparently lost for good. He would cite decisions taken, for example, to replace him in areas of work without consultation; others would remember an apparent disinclination on his part to co-operate. The team collectively remembers the difficult and painful episodes. There was no one to make the links or to challenge the 'built-in difference of behaviour' or locate its source.

Council workers came in to the project then with different job descriptions, different terms and conditions, although their accountability to the project management was defined according to a formal agreement. This was disturbing, but there was also a feeling that white colleagues were handing responsibility for black groups to the Asian workers. Yet this impression is held against the early policy of RCP that white, as well as black workers would work with black communities. The project director remembers his impression that the black workers were anxious to retain control of their work areas to the extent in one case of withholding information he considered necessary to the team as a whole. His analysis was that it was difficult for the council workers to see any advantage in working for an agency whose management and supervisory structure could possibly inhibit the methods and direction of work. Over time it was partly the resources which the project could offer to both the workers and the community groups, but also management support when workers were under pressure, which led to a different view.

The joint learning possibilities which might have been welcomed, and indeed which were in part later realised, were difficult to see at the time, particularly after the disagreements as to proposed work methods which flared in the first joint team meeting. One experienced white worker recalls standing his professional ground, 'arrogantly', he would now admit. He argued that advice work and other proposed strategies within the Asian community bore little relationship to community development. It is only retrospectively that the white worker realised that there had been a failure to take into account the long years in which at least for one of the workers as a council employee, community work had been very much an interpreting and advice role. When attacks were made on an advice role, this was in a real sense a denial of his previous experience.

The reverberations from that early clash rippled through the project in its early years, and although both black workers themselves moved away from advice work in time and could discuss such developments with individual work colleagues, constructive discussion within the team remained problematic. One worker argues: 'People were unable to acknowledge that they had moved their position, or for it to be heard when they said they no longer believed certain things. Whenever discussion became difficult we were able to move into: "Well, you don't understand."' The issue of power within the team is a crucial one. One of the black workers describes the history of the team politics in this way. 'Unless a person has some influence and is effective in the team it is difficult for him to operate in the Asian community as well. That pressure is there all the time, it depresses me, it holds me back.'

Challenging racism
The contradictions and difficulties facing a black worker joining a white-managed team were very soon apparent to the neighbourhood worker who was appointed to Cleveland Social Services as the third worker for ethnic minorities in 1984. Her job focused on supplying information about ethnic minorities to the department and increasing awareness amongst senior officers and social service practitioners. Yet, not only were there no formal structures at departmental level into which to channel and process such information, but within the team, meetings and discussion took place according to a model of community work which she perceived as designed to meet the needs of a white community. Thus, although there had been an assumption that black needs might be different, the validity of the black experience was implicitly denied. Not only was there no move to allow for difference in grass-roots experience or the black worker's practice, but the responsibility for *being heard* was placed with the worker.

Paul Stubbs refers to the general assumptions that the very

presence of black workers themselves will induce a shift in service provision (1985) and he quotes Juliet Cheetham:

Rather it was assumed that ethnic minority staff would influence white colleagues directly and indirectly in their understanding of unfamiliar cultures and the adoption of appropriate approaches to minority clients. The systems for achieving this were practically never spelt out in detail, although there were general references to shared work, direct teaching or, in the words of one optimistic area officer, simply 'being around'. (Cheetham, 1981, p. 77)

Any neighbourhood worker's job description is at best a broad one. However, the Central Middlesbrough worker was not only faced with a job description with an impossibly wide remit, but one in which the internal contradictions imposed enormous stresses and strains. What was also important were the expectations not stated in the job description. Paul Stubbs talks about the pressure on black social workers to become 'cultural experts' on terms dictated by white social workers and senior staff. Indeed, by 1986 the expectations had been codified within the job description 'to provide an in-house expertise' for the department on the needs of ethnic minority communities. More than that, the worker was required 'to contribute to any strategy developed by the department designed to combat racism', a clause which would have had more validity had it appeared in all workers' job descriptions.

Yet while on the one hand being given a strategic function, the worker was called on as an interpreter in cases such as child abuse, which were well outside her neighbourhood role, while at the same time having to resist a social work role which the community might have demanded of her. Social workers' use of the neighbourhood worker as an interpreter or translator implied that the solution to the lack of skills within their own social work teams could be found outside their own social work practice. More than that, it ensured that their own fund of knowledge and practice remained essentially unchanged.

There seems to be a problem at the interface between neighbourhood work and social planning as it relates to statutory provision. Perceiving that the real challenge was to existing concepts, practice and service delivery, the worker was left with the role of educating colleagues on their racism, which permeated the authority, ranging from the attitudes of the practitioners to that of the departmental typists. Juliet

Cheetham's observation on black social workers is relevant. They 'often felt hopelessly isolated, misunderstood, at times snubbed and overwhelmed by totally impossible administrative structures'. (1981, p. 93)

One of the ways of countering this isolation is to provide both formal and informal support sessions outside the accepted management structures. In Middlesbrough the black and white workers, both women, were able to grapple with both sexism and racism and give each other support, and they were later involved in a regional anti-racist training group, which operated as a support group and provided racism awareness training for people in community work.

In Cheetham Hill in Manchester the Al-Hilal worker was able to use the white officer from the community development section, himself previously a community worker in Cheetham Hill, as a support person rather than a superviser. The very fact that there was no management relationship meant that it was easier for ideas to be offered and shared. Moreover, the fact that the decisions to open out discussion lay with the black worker operated to counterweigh any power imbalance between them, and they were able to avoid the breakdown which can take place in supervision where a point becomes controversial.

In Rochdale, CPF by contrast was operating a more complex situation, but one in which considerations of the nature of the support given by management had been subordinated to other priorities. There had been an early decision to prioritise the links into the local authority; by doing so it had sacrificed the opportunity for other voices to be heard in the management of the project. The result was an all-white male management, some of whom were the black council secondee's own senior officers. And as the project director reflects: 'It was not just the management committee, but there were no other black significant people around. There were no Asians in prominent positions in the local authority, no one else to refer to who would offer an alternative perspective. It was either us or them.' The reference here was to the often bitter dispute about appropriate working methods, arising from a difference of approach between the black and white members of the team. Some feel now that it was not surprising that in those conditions the black workers were reluctant to bring issues to the management committee.

The formal document which clarified the secondment made it clear that workers were accountable to the management committee through the project head, while employment responsibilities remained with the planning department. However, the chief planning officer remained their senior officer and his position on the management committee placed the secondees in a potentially problematic position given the sometimes critical position of the project.

Internal support also had its own problems. One of the council workers had been working independently for some time and it was necessary to 'play it by ear'. As it was, the supervision sessions held in the early days of the project were not sustained on a regular basis, and were not satisfactory to either side. The workers could justifiably question the appropriateness of such support when management itself was unfamiliar with the dynamics of working in an Asian community. At the same time the project director felt that there were large areas which were left undiscussed and that the black workers had information and relationships which he also needed in his contact and negotiating role with the local authority.

Agencies should be aware that where they manage projects through formal hierarchies they need to put considerable thought into the role of management and provide training and support structures for managers. Grass-roots work and the social planning function are interdependent and a system which operates to cut one off from the other does not function well. The issue is particularly acute where there are white managers and black workers.

Where there are black and white workers within a team, discussion of work methods and practice becomes almost impossible if racism becomes outlawed as a subject for discussion. The reasons for this is that alternative views about the presence of racism within the agency become interwoven with personal and other differences about working methods. A pandora's box is created of unspoken distress, tensions and sheer confusion. The conflicts which take place barely scratch the surface, but get enshrined in the team's psychological history, providing a further barrier to discussion.

Yet there is a real need for workers to discuss together how racism works institutionally and there is a degree of personal commitment required to do this. Too often such discussion is linked to personal attack. As one of the Rochdale workers said: 'It becomes very difficult to raise all those things in a team meeting, you know. If one person says "I'm not racist!" how can you say "Yes you are!"'

Whites soon learn that trying to talk openly about black and white relations, and about racism, is one of the riskiest undertakings in a group with black people; keeping silent, however, is not just a way of minimising personal risk but is also a potent tool for maintaining power and control. (Thomas, 1986, p. 78)

David Thomas goes on to describe the need for white workers to confront any apprehension at working in black neighbourhoods and to recognise how such feelings affect relationships with black colleagues as well as residents. Most of the white workers in this study would agree to feeling 'frightened', when they first started work with black communities, particularly when the highly structured and apparently rigid nature of some Asian communities and the overt racism demonstrated by white residents became apparent. Some had hoped that the black workers would 'show them how to do it' and had no fallback position when the anticipated hand holding did not take place. Black workers are increasingly unwilling to be seen as 'experts' on aspects of black culture. They may also have little wish to discuss anti-racism in the context of the community until racism within the agency has been tackled.

At the same time it should be recognised that it is possible for white workers to receive a number of contradictory messages. One of the black workers in this study argued both that white workers could not be effective in working with black groups, and also accused the agency of racism because white workers were not working sufficiently with black communities. Perhaps there are inevitably conflicting feelings co-existing which give rise to such conflicting or inconsistent statements, but it must be recognised that these can be quite paralysing in their effect. The way forward from this must be for such contradictory messages to be discussed at team meetings, and for clarification of what can and cannot be delivered, at both an individual and a team level.

Professional resistance to change
The other important factors which hinder the successful tackling of racism are the ways in which notions of hierarchy and status work. Added to status founded on race is that based on sex, experience, the use of information and personality difference. Looking at the Rochdale experience, the effect of the hierarchical domination of the project by white men is evident to some of the workers in retrospect, although there

are different views. For the project head: 'It felt to me that a reverse hierarchy was in operation; most team decisions were imposed on me and individuals had tremendous space in which to develop their own work.'

One worker in Manchester can identify retrospectively how his status and white identity in the 1970s limited action and a challenge to his own perceptions, reflecting that both he and others accepted too easily the role assigned to him: 'Had there been less acceptance, we might have got into more fruitful discussion about what was community work and what it had to offer, but the fact that I was working for the local authority and was prepared to talk to people in their own houses was received as wonderful.' In Rochdale, too, it is possible to see how white senior workers, while admitting to ignorance of the black experience and a willingness to be guided, at the same time used a narrow view of community work skills to resist any challenge to their own priorities and perceptions, using both accepted community work practice and project objectives as ammunition.

All three white male community workers had a strong personal motivation for joining RCP. Although attracted to work in multi-racial areas, what had drawn them to the project was the focus on resident involvement in urban renewal within the context of a time-limited rolling programme. As against much community work which was often open-ended, it seemed that it might be possible to define certain clear objectives and to be able to move on when they were attained. This commitment to the perceived obejctives was reinforced by the pressure to work in more 'safe' areas, and it is clear that the pressures to accept other methods and a less rigid approach were experienced as the same thing. Indeed, the confusion was reinforced by the close relationship which had existed between one of the black workers and the CBAA co-ordinator and the legitimate points became lost in the confusion.

For the white workers it was frustrating then to hear the black workers in the team say at any early stage that working within the housing brief was not so direct a process. For them the path to resident involvement in urban renewal and decision making was not a straight one, but involved many detours, through advice sessions and broad-based community schemes, and necessitated the negotiating of power politics and interest groups. Furthermore, they were later to argue that the timescale of involvement could not be determined by the progress made by the CBAA offices, but guided by the internal demands for support and slow withdrawal.

One of the other blocks in discussing strategy was the differing viewpoints of the two black workers; indeed the potential always existed for the approach and actions of one to undermine the field work of the other, given their separate work with groups who were often in open conflict on a town-wide scale. This may seem an inevitable danger in community work teams, and one which requires open resolution. One of the team reflects:

While these differences were often buried, the closer we got to a real discussion of strategy the more important and more damaging it would have become; it undoubtedly added an extra 'spin' to the situation, and one the importance of which it is difficult to over-estimate. Management wasn't really equipped to deal with it, and the dominant traditional white philosophy and practice could not relate to it.

Shifts in attitudes and perspectives
Several factors caused a gradual shift in position within RCP. As the urban aid for the projects materialised there was an increasing interest shown by council officers and CPF; the project 'seemed to fit' with current interests. Secondly, the project objectives as a whole, which had originally been defined in narrow terms of housing and environmental issues, were broadened for other reasons. Thirdly, the timescale no longer seemed a major determinant in maintaining the professional focus which they had desired.

However both black workers have bitter memories of working to the point where there was a shift in attitude. One worker points out that, newly trained, and unable to find literature which would support his position, he felt that the onus of proof lay with him, forcing him to put extraordinary hours and effort into the field work. He describes his early work in Wardleworth and Sparthbottoms as 'hell', and 'I felt that I was feeling my own way and at the same time I had to educate my colleagues. For the first two years it was a very agonising period for me.'

What is required in this situation is a recognition of different spheres of experience and competence, a willingness by white workers to value the skills and understanding which they often acknowledge that they do not have themselves. This two-way process of mutual trust and respect can be done only in an atmosphere where claims to expertise and professional competence do not block dialogue and where discussion is based on co-operation rather than competition.

Even co-operation can be painful. In Middlesbrough the black and white neighbourhood workers worked closely together. They feel that their arrival at a position of mutual support might not have been possible but for several factors: a racism awareness training course had clarified issues for both of them; and above all they were both committed to what was often time-consuming and difficult discussion of problems encountered not just in their work practice but in their joint working. They also feel that as two women they were better able to resolve the difficulties together. In other situations we have seen that joint working across the sexes has had both its problems and successes. Personality factors certainly play their part; what is vital is a commitment to discuss and resolve issues as they arise.

In these situations workers may feel they are walking through a minefield, and indeed they must be prepared for some painful episodes in order to arrive at a situation where discussion can be open without causing personal distress. The white worker had to learn to use her greater familiarity with the basic philosophy of community development in a way that was useful to both of them; for the black worker there was a sense of frustration with language which was often non-specific and ambiguous. The white worker had also to confront her tendency to assume that her black colleagues had an exhaustive knowledge of Asians, while at the same time she needed to fight a contradictory tendency to be the more vocal in meetings, to take the lead, being seen as an 'expert' on black issues and 'deskilling' the black worker.

Within RCP, apart from any practical considerations of maximising skills there was an ideological motivation to work in partnership between black and white workers for its 'demonstration effect' of co-existence and co-operative and productive working. Despite the major difficulties within the team, for the two workers working together in Sparth there were areas where it was possible to develop discussion both informally and with the help of the project director if things were difficult, enabling a joint strategy for the community centre or for separate development. Their specific joint remit certainly made a joint strategy easier; a joint working knowledge of the particular area was critical in leading to shared perceptions.

In that situation, where there is partnership working there needs to be a readiness to look at conflicting motivation and styles and to develop a framework where perceptions can be explored and interact rather than compete. Several years later the black worker was working closely with one of the women team members. They set up regular planning sessions, exploring things that had worked well and any particular differences between them. 'Talking about things all the time', they recognised each other's strengths and encouraged each other in areas of weakness, working hard at not allowing differences of gender and race to be disruptive. Her interpretation was that they shared a position 'at the bottom of the status hierarchy in the team'. This is not a shared team perception; less debateable was that personality factors and an understanding of their joint potential were vital to overcoming difficulties.

Nevertheless the experience within the team had been that endless arguments were held about whether community work in black communities was different to that practised in white neighbourhoods. The arguments never seemed to develop to a point at which the considerable work experience could be properly assessed. To the black workers the sense of powerlessness within the team was paramount, the reasons for those early barriers incomprehensible. It seemed that they were in a situation where those who could shout loudest or were most familiar with the process and willing to write up their projects in the language of community development would be heard. The reality was that all workers were pressed to write up their work and there were continual requests to talk at CPF seminars, particularly on housing and urban renewal. However, the demands of community development do not make such additional work easy, and where there is individual dissatisfaction or dissent this may well dampen enthusiasm to expound a project's achievements.

A responsive and dynamic project management in relation to the promotion of learning opportunities is essential. What appears to be open argument can co-exist with what is effectively closed debate where the atmosphere is defensive and competitive and the overriding concern of individuals is to maintain positions of power and influence. In such an atmosphere, even where views change, myths about respectively held positions can be stronger than reality and a cycle of distrust can be established where workers are unable to approach each other for advice or even information. Where the only status afforded the black worker is derived from her knowledge of black communities, the appropriate reaction may well be to hold that information close; where the norm does not change, it might feel less threatening to work outside the structures. Conflicting strategies, even a split team, are only a logical consequence of such a situation. There may be elements in the community work ethos which encourage these styles, an individualistic approach and a reluctance to admit to uncertainty or ignorance. In RCP, even when there was a gradual shift in views towards an acceptance of the black workers' methodology, this was signalled by a falling away of opposition rather than open acknowledgement. It would have helped, as one worker said, if there had been some open recognition. Again the community work ethos is to be self-critical and to deny the worker's part in a group's 'success'. This raises real problems in relation to valuing the individual's work. As the RCP project director recognises now: 'I never realised that people needed some tangible form of recognition to the extent that they did.'

Personal interpretation and what appeared sometimes to be a devaluing of each other's work might have been avoided if there had been team ownership. Possibly this would have been achieved if they had written up a monthly work-sheet for internal team discussion. Certainly it should have provided a learning process for the individual and a pooling of experience and skills learnt, and would have provided a useful basis for evaluation. However, it is unusual for community projects to have evaluation sessions unless there is a particular brief. Managers do not always have the specialist skills required, and an imaginative use of alternative resources and outside facilitators could be used to advantage.

Guidelines for the future

The appointment of workers

Possibly there are key criteria for appointment of community workers: that they should be open, sufficiently strong to confront their own assumptions and sufficiently flexible to step outside what might be a fashionable model and to work in different ways. What an agency should be looking for in all workers is an ability to reflect on past experiences and practice in a way which enables the individual to move into new situations and confront dominant community work models where necessary.

There needs to be careful consideration of matching of the worker to the needs of the community; this must depend on both the nature of the community and the important issues. The Al-Hilal project, for example emphasises the importance of the women workers' input to the development of work with young girls and women and also the conditional nature of the community's trust in such workers. As the project's first women youth worker commented: 'The worker couldn't come in with a bad reputation – the girls wouldn't come. I was doing everything the community wanted. They accepted it because everything I was doing was Islamically based.' Indeed in South Manchester, where a broader range of work has been possible, the experience remains similar. One woman, a local authority community development officer, found that it was difficult for some men to accept her because of her previous work in the women's refuge.

On the other hand, in Cleveland, where in many respects the Asian community reflects most closely the traditions of rural Pakistan, two workers there are anxious to break down stereotypes of women alone being able to work with Asian women. Certainly appointing a woman as such does not necessarily answer the problems, nor is it always appropriate to look primarily to appoint from the 'target' ethnic group, even where this may be legally possible. Not only can this deny the importance of other personality factors, but it can lead to defining the required group identity in increasingly narrow terms. The Afro-Caribbean worker in Cheetham Hill felt that part of the value of his position lay not just in his adaptability, a willingness to concentrate his efforts on what the community wanted, but that, while not Asian, nor Muslim, as a black worker he would be seen less as part of the power structure. He too suffered as a result of the norm.

For the worker, her particular ethnic identity will carry with it varying realities according to circumstance, area and community; although language ability can be crucial, it is one variable among many. Generalisations are misleading but there are lessons to be learnt from particular instances. When one black worker started work in Manchester, living outside his area of work, attempts were made quickly to 'locate' him; once identified, he was on that basis both granted and refused access to certain groups in a way that gave him only limited room to manoeuvre. One of the important factors was the support offered to enable him to work effectively.

A woman worker, an Urdu speaker, found that in working with the Punjabi community in Cleveland, the language difficulties did not become important. Although she was treated as an outsider, it was without hostility and in some ways operated to her advantage in her dealings with men in the community. However, she does feel that in that particular community, it is all-important for an Asian worker to be Muslim. Her work had previously been in London. 'I never thought about all this in London,' she says, 'but here there is a lot of bitterness between Hindus and Muslims and because of the highly religious way of life they expect you to understand them if you are going to work with them.'

The workers who have contributed to this study have by no means an identical perception of the critical issues. In the Manchester Community Development team, gender is often perceived as crucial in work with women. The feeling is that women workers are more responsive to issues which are specific to women and are able to progress faster than male workers would on issues such as women and health. The way such work is perceived in the community is also seen as important; it is felt that in certain sensitive areas the presence of male workers might meet with disapproval and withdrawal of support.

Another worker believes that the desire for workers within the community's own social, religious and language groups is a healthy one and should not be avoided; indeed that workers should be recruited from the groups themselves as far as possible and that agencies should avoid recruiting outsiders. However, her definition of an 'outsider' needs to be defined more clearly. She herself is an Punjabi Hindu, but feels that she shares with the Pakistani Muslim women she works with a language and rural background, the culture of peasant communities. Her perception is that a white woman who knows the language and culture would nevertheless be more appropriate than someone from the same area, but whose higher status in the community would intrude, reproducing the dominance pattern of the rural hierarchies. In working with social groups which are displaced from rural societies there is a continuum from a situation where the landowner is the only literate person. The emergence of the leader in urban British society with social welfare functions replicates the class divisions of rural India and Pakistan. She feels that with such a person it may not be possible to move forward on crucial issues such as tackling racism in an urban environment.

Furthermore, it must be recognised that the concept of community is a dynamic one, and the realities of working with British-educated Asians different. Life in Britain, unemployment, low incomes and inadequate living conditions affect the household, the woman's place in it, the real identity of the children, gradually changing the concept of what it means to be a Pakistani or an Indian. Agencies must understand and work with those realities.

Christopher Ensor, Ismail Lambat and Duncan Scott pursue these points in the following way:

There is no easy, right answer to the question of finding the worker with the most suitable background to work in a multi-ethnic area. Much depends on the previous experience and style of intervention as well as his or her ethnic credentials and the nature of the area and any particular target populations. Obviously it makes sense to look for a worker who has a good understanding of the issues affecting a target population and the ability to communicate and build up trust with the people. This will often point to a worker with the same ethnic background as the target population. However this in itself will not necessarily make the worker more effective. We have shown how divisions within ethnic groups at a local level make the position of the worker extremely difficult. If he or she has close links with the factions involved or, more difficult still, comes from one of the factions, effectiveness can be severely limited. (1982)

It also occurs that in chasing the 'right' religion, or skin colour, or social group, agencies may forget the personal qualities and skills that will make for a successful appointment. If, for example, an ability to work closely with a partner or in a team is essential, it should be made a criterion for appointment, and it is fair neither to the agency nor to the individual if these factors are overlooked.

The experience of Manchester has been that in recent appointments of neighbourhood workers to work in multi-racial areas, greater value has been placed on qualifications such as an understanding of racism and work with black groups. In this situation recognition must be given if, as has happened, appointees do not have the background which would give them prior knowledge of other areas such as local authority structures. The content and method of induction training may have to be reassessed, although there is a point where on-the-job experience must take over from formal training. Access to training should ideally be available at a time when it is required by the worker in order for it to be effective. Certainly the amount of time and financial resources set aside for support, supervision and even consultancy should be carefully considered.

Management

In a more complex bureaucracy, it is even more crucial that managers are aware of the worker's needs. They must recognise the need to support the workers, both black and white, when there are attempts from within the community to control them as well as pressures which derive from within the agency. There is a very real sense in which the mistakes of managers add to the difficulties of workers if, for example, they have not understood why certain approaches or complaints have been made to them by community leaders. The workers in this study have experienced attempts by community leaders to force them to abandon areas of work where those leaders have felt their own position threatened by change or increasing power held by new community activists. There have been petitions against community workers, complaints to politicians and chief officers, even physical attack. As one worker expressed it, 'If we knew that management support would not be forthcoming, I doubt whether we would have dared to embark on certain areas of work.'

Managers must be sensitive to issues which concern hierarchies and status within teams and communities, experienced acutely by the women in this study, which may overlay or compound racism. Supervision and support sessions need to provide a framework within which the workers can clarify objectives and working methods against other models, a space in which experiences can be tested. A manager would add that

The atmosphere must also be created where black workers' practice can also be questioned constructively by white colleagues and supervisers without black workers being defensive. I think that in some cases now white managers and colleagues, in attempting to be aware, non-racist etc. can find it difficult or even impossible to question and challenge the work practice and ideology of some strong black workers.

It should be understood that the less supported a worker feels, the greater the likelihood of a defensive approach. Constructive support may be hampered at the outset by an inability to empathise with the isolation of a black worker in institutions where there may be few other black workers, let alone black senior officers, and a failure to understand the kinds of pressures to which black workers are subject. Without confronting those issues the manager may feel insecure and lack confidence in the legitimacy of her or his supervisory role. For the projects officer in Cleveland there was a sense of moving into uncharted areas, and it was some time before the levels of anxiety on both sides were sufficiently reduced to permit a measure of trust and learning.

As with discussions between black and white workers, there must be an awareness of how power positions and 'white-dominated models' provide barriers to acquiring alternative perceptions of work methods.

We use this term with grave reservations, having engaged in much lengthy discussion about what it really meant. One view within the group was that a 'white model' of community development, for example, did not exist. Yet it is difficult to dismiss the term as meaningless when it was used, almost without exception, by everyone interviewed. One interviewee, talking about training provision, when challenged, said: 'In white institutions everything is presented in a very formal manner. Maybe we should be talking about doing something which is suited to the ordinary person, rather than the professional; we are talking about starting from where they are.' Perhaps, then, we are simply referring to 'inappropriate' models. However, this usage does not indicate that the norm often fails to reflect a black perspective, something which is indicated by the shorthand term 'white model'.

Discussion should take place collectively about whether differences in work approach are valid, rather than wait for crisis incidents. Often the difficulty arises from lack of mutual trust, on the one hand that the worker's reasoning is sound and on the other that the supervisor has credibility or some valid experience on which to base judgements, and that there is an awareness of the very real additional pressures that the black workers may be under from both communities and from white colleagues. Solutions need to be sought which place a value on assessing experience and on management, whether that management operates through hierarchies or collectives. Agencies also need to ensure that there are black people in key management, worker and support positions. However, there seems to be no reason why white managers should feel they have nothing to offer. There will be differences of experience and approach just as there are differences reflected amongst those who have contributed to this study; the mutual challenge and dialogue is vital.

Yet there is a real danger of losing sight of the role and value of supervision or support sessions, whether they are conducted through a collective team or a project leader. In Cleveland, for example, both individual supervision and project meetings between principal and divisional officers and neighbourhood workers became a casualty of decentralisation, leading to a loss of direction and a decreased ability to plan and evaluate work.

Clearly there is a need for agencies, and their project managers and workers, to understand and recognise the context of racism within which they are working. Models of community work are being operated which are based on assumptions of services and facilities available to white communities within the neighbourhood, which may not be accessible to all. For example, the use of a room above a pub may be available as a community facility for white groups but quite inappropriate for a Muslim group. The use of libraries and schools, apparently provided for everyone, may not seem impossible, but they are perceived as white-dominated institutions and specific initiatives are required to alter that reality. Particular thought needs to be given to access to resources by Asian women, who may be able to use facilities in certain circumstances only. There is often an assumption that there is a support network operating effectively within the neighbourhood. For black communities this assumption is invalid. Council workers often focus on the language barrier, and fail to understand how the infrastructure of services bypasses black people.

It is essential then that an alternative perspective is built in at management level to validate the black workers' experience, through training for existing managers, the employment of black and white workers, in key posts and management positions, who understand black communities and the nature and operation of racism, and the provision of support from the black communities themselves.

6 Crisis of Accountability: The Worker between the Agency and the Community

The community work tightrope

We have noted that there are different notions of accountability. For some it may represent the tensions deriving from a sense of duty, for others a responsiveness to needs, and for others the obligations to a funder or sponsor. If real accountability can be measured in terms of its effectiveness then one must look for evidence of mechanisms whereby such accountability can be exerted. These structures usually exist between worker and employer and colleagues. However, in Manchester there have been attempts to define accountability to the community, and to understand how it might become a workable reality. The city council requested departments to put forward proposals for approval which would act on and develop requirements for section 11 workers to be accountable to the community. The community development section decided that this notion of accountability should affect not just section 11 workers but the whole section. Initially, community groups have been involved in appointments to posts, although in an advisory position, given that the workers' contract remains with the SSD. It has been proposed that reports on work should be made to the community groups. Logically this would lead to such reports being drawn up in consultation with the community, substantially altering the nature of the relationship.

For the local authority worker there may be a real sense of contradictory pressure between the needs of the community and the agency. A Somali worker employed by the local authority to work with the Somali community in Cleveland felt she was often 'walking a tightrope'; she was aware that she found it particularly difficult to be open with the agency about anything which would reflect disadvantageously on the community.

However, this prime responsibility to the employer, particularly where it is the local authority, may make the groups distrust the worker. Black workers in Cleveland and Manchester record pressure on them to achieve things for groups which are entirely out of their control; coming to terms with the reality is a slow, painful process for the worker and for the groups. If black workers are indeed under greater pressure to 'come up with the goods', then they are being increasingly placed in an untenable position, given the scarcity of resources, unless there is the political will locally to do something about redistributing available resources so that black communities receive their equitable share. The position is not promising: in none of the areas in our study are black communities in the position where the black vote would be considered critical by political parties. In Manchester in 1987 only three of the 99 councillors were black; it would be naive to think that black groups are in a position to directly affect policies through pressure on the voting system. Indeed, to the contrary, in Manchester the Labour Party, with its massive majority of seats, is only too aware of the possible backlash against some of the council equal opportunities initiatives.

Furthermore, to the extent that black representatives on local councils take a line which is different from that of the dominant party group, they may well find their influence declines, putting them in a relatively powerless position in terms of representing particular black interests. Marian Fitzgerald (1987) points to the common response of the main political parties to the urban disturbances of 1981 and 1985 to deracialise the issues. Within the left of the Labour Party a colour blindness relates to fundamentalist socialism which argues the paramountcy of class as overriding all other divisions.

Already, particularly in local government, the latter have begun to face conflict between socialist principles and those of ethnic pluralism; their commitments to a range of very diverse minority rights even within a clear socialist framework is beginning to generate dilemmas (highlighted by the opposition by some black groups to the left's commitment on gay rights). (p. 46)

In analysing the Rochdale experience we have seen workers stand in different relationships to the community, and derive often quite divergent approaches from their respective positions. Yet similar tensions may exist even where the goals and outlook of the community, agency and worker appear to coincide. The Al-Hilal worker felt that his involvement in the Muslim parents' campaign for single sex education for local Muslim girls was of a nature quite different from the involvement of a white worker 'doing something for ethnic minorities'; the work concerned the survival of his own value system. Yet the pulls and tensions he experienced in defining his role and function between the community, the agency and his funder, the local authority, were a dominant part of that experience.

In the mid-1970s, he had been chairman of the local mosque and involved in local community activities in the area. In 1977 he started to work with the community association, teaching young children Arabic. Thus when he started working with the newly formed Al-Hilal Community Project, he was already well-established in the area as a key figure. Moreover, during this time the worker was chairman of the ward Labour Party and general secretary of the UK Islamic Mission. This needs to be qualified; this web of influence and interest brought as much opposition as it brought support. The worker, with an urban background, had a particular, and to some extent a limited, power base. We have referred previously to the existence within Cheetham Hill of a rival Muslim organisation hostile to the project which was attached to the more wealthy, influential mosque, and which drew its leadership from the middle class men who had come from a small landowning background in Pakistan. Moreover there are particular issues raised by a use of the Labour Party to promote the interests not just of the worker's community but of his particular group. The danger of blurring the distinction between being a paid worker of the Al-Hilal project and being a Manchester citizen with a legitimate political interest and a right to express it, was that it became difficult for others to recognise his role at any given time.

Initially, then, it seemed important to separate the work with the girls' education issue from the Al-Hilal Project. This was achieved by drawing the parents of the girls affected by educational reorganisation into the apparently neutral Muslim Parents' Association (MPA), and to conduct negotiations with the local authority through that organisation. However, in the event this put the worker in a difficult position.

In August 1982, places were offered at a single sex school in South Manchester, but this was not accompanied by an offer of transport to carry the girls through the centre of the city. Sixteen girls were withdrawn and went on school attendance strike and their parents were threatened with court action. The community and the Muslim Parents' Association urged the worker to adopt a more strident approach.

However, the worker remained accountable to Al-Hilal, a local authority-funded project, which had a management committee which included the local councillor involved in much of the negotiation between the MPA and the local authority, as well as representatives from the social services and education department. The Muslim representatives were concerned about the future funding of the project while some Manchester City officers were of the view that when the parents withdrew the children from school, the worker's role should be to stop the parents from breaking the law and to ensure that the children returned to school. Outsiders were in a small but powerful minority on the management committee, and did not always agree among themselves. The social services representative was better placed than that of the education department to be more supportive to alternative and intermediate solutions, such as interim classes, while the children were on school strike. Against a background of warning about 'carrying on like this in this country' and 'the regrettable attitude you and your community have adopted', the worker felt trapped between the pressures of the local community and the local authority which provided the project funding.

In an attempt to break the deadlock, and without the approval of either the MPA or the project, the worker held a series of confidential meetings with senior staff in the education department. By the early autumn of 1983, following an agreement by the department to provide transport to the South Manchester school and the promise that recommendations would be made to alter the allocation system in North Manchester, the worker persuaded the community to drop the campaign.

It was an enormous blow to the parents when the education committee decided against accepting the recommendations to alter the allocation system. It also called into question the role of the community worker. On the one hand part of his objective had been that people should become familiar with British institutions and ways of operating without losing their own Muslim identity. To some extent that objective had been met. A small group of parents had been closely involved with the negotiations with the council, and were bitter about the outcome. But more than this, large numbers of the community had campaigned for the first time for their rights; they were becoming aware of a society which did not take account of their concerns or understand their needs.

From this point the conclusions drawn were quite distinct. While some community members would agree with the worker that their interests should be pursued further through continued community work and through black people entering and participating in democratic institutions, for many there was a reaffirmation that a more confrontational approach should have been followed.

The position of the community worker in this case has several points of similarity with the middleperson or 'middleman' role identified by Gerry Stoker and Tim Brindley in Leicester City politics (1985). Such a role, they argue, arises where there are major discontinuities in the total hierarchy, where there is a gap in information flow, cultural incomprehension and a conflict of values and interests. The 'middleman' faces a number of difficulties:

On the one hand, although the middleman may be able to establish a leadership role within the subordinate structure he is likely to be in a marginal position with respect to the superior structure. The middleman is usually found at the lower end of the hierarchy of structure A. This can severely threaten his ability to 'deliver the goods' for the subordinate structure B. On the other hand, the middleman is likely to be subjected to severe cross-acting pressures.

They add that the 'middleman' runs the risk of being branded a renegade, or a traitor, or most commonly as an unprincipled man on the make.

Ismail Lambat (Scott et al. 1981), working with another group of Muslim parents on the question of physical education dress in a school in a small Yorkshire town describes himself as somewhere between the agency that employed him, the local authority, and the people he was employed to work with, often feeling suspected by both. For the Al-Hilal worker, branded as an agitator by council officers and as in the pocket of councillors by some of the parents, the position was a similarly uncomfortable one.

Local authority employees
The local authority employee may feel yet more compromised in her position than the local authority-funded worker in a non-statutory agency. Local authority departments are generally

looking for relatively 'safe' projects in multi-ethnic areas around education and play, regarding a campaigning position as incon- sistent with the desired 'neutrality' of council officers, or indeed with the expectation that officers will actively support council or departmental policy. The community worker will also find her- self up against a rigid application of departmental procedures which may make almost impossible the high profile approach, for example the use of the media, and the ability to cut corners necessary for example in immigration and deportation cases. The visibility of the worker herself, particularly in an area where the local authority is itself the target of action or criticism, is of crucial importance.

Where departmental policies and services are involved, not all council officers will appreciate a critical approach by the worker. Indeed, council officers may try to hamper independent critical action, and open criticism, by appealing to group loyalty. Elizabeth Filkin and Michael Naish (1982), referring to attempts by employers to intervene where direct and positive support to certain community groups is perceived as a threat to the employers' interests, cite methods which might include anger, coolness, threats, or blandishments, and suggest that an early clarification of job descriptions by workers is essential.

In these circumstances, the worker may well feel justified in avoiding 'support' or supervision sessions. Without a basis of trust and shared objectives the worker may feel better able to change the perceptions of departmental colleagues and senior officers through independent work. At the very least they may feel able to work as they see best without interference. For the black employee, often viewed as a link between the council and the black community, used for translating, information and interpreting purposes, the position can be even more difficult. Within the community the worker may well be working against an unrealistic expectation of what can be obtained through local government, whether in terms of resources or changed policy. This may be based on a lack of knowledge of local government structures and processes.

The Cleveland workers would argue that there is a difference between the demands made by the black and white communi- ties. They feel that what is demanded by white communities is control of the information and the agency, but that the black communities demand to know what the worker is doing *for* the community. The tension here lies in the demands of self-determination and the community worker's ideal of a demo-cratising process within communities. The concern by workers is that where the community focus is on religion, there are few other ways of learning organisational skills. Further, where links are through mosque leaders, the information may well stop there.

The Somali worker in Cleveland, coming from within her community, and previously involved with the Somali Com-munity Association, found nevertheless that she did have a different agenda from that of the men, those visible and vocal in the community, and experienced attempts by them to control her work. For the worker, the demands of community develop-ment went beyond a preoccupation with obtaining a place of worship and other religious concerns. These were the priorities of the men who made up the association's committee, but she felt were not the prime or only concerns of the women in the community, nor of the second generation Somalis. Indeed, she felt that the men, very much the spokespeople for the com-munity, could not represent the needs of what was a very diverse community.

It is difficult for the community worker to be clear in this situation. A community centre warden in Rochdale insists that there should be continual checks that the workers are referring to the objectives of the community and not to their own values, but she adds, 'How do you deal with each group thinking thier own issues are a priority?' The reality is that the concept of community development in itself posits a set of core values which may not sit easily with certain expressed demands. 'Community accountability' can become glib and meaningless when a worker is faced with a plethora of needs put forward by different communities, sometimes in a volatile and mutually hostile or exclusive way.

The myth of neutrality
In Rochdale the internal history of the Milkstone Residents' Association and the Castlemere Community Centre serves to demonstrate the vulnerability of the community worker. Pro-posals for a community centre had been put forward by the residents' association in association with the mosque committee in response to the availability of an empty building in late 1981.

By the time the centre had received funding approval following a second application towards the end of 1982, rival groups had formed in the residents' association and become preoccupied with a struggle for positions of power both within the residents' association and on the executive committee of the Council for Racial Equality (CRE). As both the mosque and local politicians became involved, a breakaway and rival association was formed, while interest groups radiating out from the residents' association became enmeshed in the interests of the political parties. The steering group for the proposed community centre provided further occasion for the competing factions to argue with each other. By autumn 1983, the chairman of the residents' association, a shopowner and politician who had successfully used the residents' association as a power base, had been challenged and replaced by a younger man who had the backing of the Liberal Party.

The worker had seen his role as one in which he worked with whatever group appeared operational at any given time. He found that in a situation of conflict, such a position was not a viable one. In April 1983, a split had occurred in the mosque committee and by mid-1981 there was an accusation that the worker had been interfering with the affairs of the mosque. It was necessary for RCP to assert neutrality at an official level, and relationships at one stage deteriorated to such an extent that it became increasingly difficult for the worker to maintain contact with each group and to carry out his community work function. There was a danger that the bitterness between the two groups, fully reported in the local press, would deflect the attention of those groups from local housing and environmental issues.

It also became apparent that it would be impossible for him to maintain his neutral role. Feeling unable to go out, because he could not be seen with either group, he at one stage confined himself to his room. He did make an attempt at mediation, bringing in the local MP to chair a meeting. With the failure of this attempt, and as the opposing faction, strongly identified with the Liberal Party, gained control, it became impossible for the worker to continue to walk what was effectively a political tightrope. His very enabling role identified him come what may with the successful faction. The project director, writing to CPF in June 1983, declared that while the worker felt able to cope with the reaction locally, it was also felt important, given the obvious political overtones, that the project let it be known 'that we are not prepared to let ourselves be portrayed as favouring either side'.

However, that identification at a time of contest and crisis was hard to shake, and when Labour gained control of the borough council in the elections of 1986, and there was a parallel change in control in the Milkstone Residents' Association, complaints were raised about political bias; to the worker it felt as though politicians were trying to restrict community action for their own benefit.

The black worker in the Wardleworth area of Rochdale found himself in a very similar situation. A Bangladeshi, it was within the Bangladeshi community that the problems of maintaining a perceived neutrality became most acute. In his position as secretary to the new Bangladesh Community Project, the worker was able to involve members of the Bangladesh Association who had previously carried little influence, some of whom were unemployed textile workers. Attending meetings, lobbying and learning skills, this group grew in confidence, and it was this group which challenged the previously uncontested position of the chair of the Bangladesh Association.

After a fraught election of community association officers, in which the ballot box was held in police custody overnight, the chairman was replaced for the first time not by someone with financial or political influence, but by a 'nobody in the Bangladesh community – someone elected just because he was interested'. But if this was beginning to be a trend in Rochdale community politics, so too was the intermeshing of mosque, community group and party political affairs. Again it proved too potent a combination for the worker to remain unaffected. The previous chairman had regarded the worker's support as unconditional; when it appeared not to be so, again complaints were made to the council about alleged political bias. 'Neutrality' had once more proved elusive, and was to prove increasingly so. Even where utmost care was taken not to be seen to be working with one group, the intersection of interest and involvement in the community was such that it was almost impossible not to avoid group identification. Even working with the residents' association, familiarising members with the council committee system, meant that such information could be used for small group interests, and the inference could be made that the worker was supporting that group. As the inter-group competition for resources intensified, the possibility of scapegoating the worker in the case of non-delivery became an increasing hazard, the reality being that there were fewer resources to offer anybody.

These problems are not new within community work. Access to groups is essentially through personal contact. Resentment among individuals and groups as a result of apparent selective interest and attention is also familiar, and should not in itself be the reason for avoiding choices. However, there is a pivotal role played by local parties in Asian community politics which provides an important dimension. British local government politics has developed from a tradition of support gained from special interest and promise of rewards. However, there are features of local politics in its relation to black communities which have a specific bearing on community work, and the next chapter will illustrate how far this is true in our areas of study. The particular details relate to those localities; the political reality is that a local party candidate will perceive race issues differently where the ward contains a 6 per cent black vote to one in which it is 60 per cent. The circumstances of a London borough and inner Rochdale may be quite different; some of the elements within it may not be.

7 The Political Context: Parties and Power Struggles

Although every community worker experiences community activity in its relationship to local and national politics, much community development theory denies this reality through its silence on the political context. The history of community development over two decades has been in many ways one of retreat. Central government reacted to the political connections which had been made by community development workers in the 1970s between poverty and structural inequalities by shutting down many community development projects. Local authority departments in particular moved away from what were perceived as 'dangerous' associations with grass-roots development, away from concepts of 'community work' and into 'neighbourhood work', concentrating on its connections with social planning. Some textbook writers have colluded with a vision of community development which denies the connections which must be made to political decisions taken at the national and local level and which dominate economic and social life at a neighbourhood level. Moreover, community work in the context of black groups reveals a particular relationship to party politics not found in the white community for several reasons. Among these are the racism operating within political parties, the exploitation of community leadership, and the particular nature of political wheeler-dealing, the 'block vote' bargained against the promise of resources, and finally the operation of consultation procedures with black communities.

Limits of radical acceptance
In the campaign for single sex education for Muslim girls in North Manchester the Al-Hilal worker had been able to mobilise support through his influence on three fronts: religious, political

and professional. The result was impressive support from all the mosques in the city, with Muslims of all communities uniting in a demonstration outside the town hall. Through his chairmanship of the Cheetham Labour Party, six North Manchester wards were mobilised and support gained from the local Member of Parliament. The Muslim Parents' Association also had the support of the community workers' forum, the community associaton, the advice centre and the local headteachers.

Yet when the chief education officer presented recommendations that there should be two single sex schools within the area, his paper was thrown out. When the crucial vote was taken in the council chamber there were only two votes backing the Muslim Parents' Association. They had counted on at least 30 votes. How had they miscalculated to such an extent?

In fact the odds were against the campaign from the outset. Although the Asian vote was an important one for the Cheetham Ward councillors, there was little fear by South Manchester Labour councillors that they would lose the vote of their constituency Muslims whatever the outcome. In the rest of North Manchester, with relatively few black households, although no powerful racist lobby was mobilised, the politics of racism played its part. In the presence of manifest racism Labour councillors were anxious to avoid issues which would reveal ideological differences with their electorates. One comment on the political scene is 'that what was crucial was what were often racist councillors in mainly white areas'. In the north-east none of the councillors were prepared to concede the principle that local girls should be refused places at the neighbourhood schools to allow Muslim girls to attend. Significantly, both the leader of the council at that time and the then chair of the education committee represented that area.

But the reasons for the outcome were still more complex. In many ways the council's decisions on the issue derived from Labour Party ideology and policy making which remained insulated against and unresponsive to the campaign. The Muslim Parents' Association saw their ward councillor, a founder member of Al-Hilal and apparently sympathetic to the issues, as their key to a change in policy. The councillor herself, while presenting the views of her constituents as fairly as possible, was nevertheless wedded to the policies of a socialist council which did not perceive the demands of the Muslim community as either legitimate or as priorities in terms of the council's equal opportunities policy, indeed which saw that they possibly stood in contradiction to that policy.

Educational equal opportunity was defined as educating girls 'in the same ways as boys'; single sex education appeared to run counter to this objective. Further, the education committee had fought hard for acceptance of primary school reorganisation to feed into neighbourhood secondary schools. Defending what was relatively new policy was an absolute priority for the Labour Group. The Muslim girls issue was regarded as a further if relatively minor obstacle, given that the Conservatives and Liberals were holding wards in South Manchester and had fought successfully to exempt three prestigious schools from the feeder scheme. For the council, discussion on the single sex question had always centred on the 'technicality' of providing transport to their second choice school across town. However, the principle behind the campaign – that the girls had a right to single sex education and that the school should have been declared a special school – had never been accepted nor allowed to challenge the principle of the feeder scheme. Moreover when the council moved to the left after the city council elections in 1984, the council's policy on equal opportunities was strengthened. Ironically, the Muslim position became weaker.

The Cheetham Hill campaign had suffered considerably and the arguments been further clouded by an issue which was separate, but which became publicly linked. The Al-Hilal community worker had become involved in an attempt to establish a sixth form course for Asian girls at the Margaret Ashton College, where he was a parent governor. This move had met with substantial opposition from feminists and Asian women from South Manchester, spearheaded by the Asian Women's Movement which had the support of the Pakistani Workers' Association and the Asian Youth and Community Workers' Association. These groups attacked the assumptions behind the proposal and the educational value of a segregated course. At the same time the initiative was being challenged from within the Cheetham community by the Cheetham Asian Women's Action Group, led by the youth worker of the girls' project, who visited and discussed the issues with parents, and leafleted and lobbied councillors against the proposal.

A consultation meeting was held in the mosque to convince

the education committee that the women wanted the course. Some one hundred women, two councillors, and a woman teacher from the college met separately, while the men, the school governors and the deputy education officer met, listening to the women over the microphone.

The meeting, as well as the issue itself, raised several questions. For some, the nature of the meeting itself was descriptive. Many of the women were seen as being present in response to the call from the mosque, and were willing to 'put their hands up in the air without understanding what the issues were'. Moreover, 'a majority of the women were not used to public speaking and clearly the English atmosphere of conducting the meeting with the chairperson and the guests seated on a row of chairs whilst the women and girls squatted on the floor was not conducive to an equal debate'.

However, the objections which were being raised by some of the women were effectively voiced, although the Al-Hilal worker would argue that those voting against the course were all from South Manchester or non-Muslim. Whatever the case, the public rejection by some Asian women of the influence and intervention of male elders over women's lives was attractive to socialist councillors and branded the worker as reactionary and sexist. Following the consultation meeting the chair of the education policy committee said the objections of the women would now be discussed and that the new left-wing leadership in the council would have to reconcile its various principles; sexual and racial equality and self-determination for racial groups.

Despite opposition to the sixth form college initiative, which did not go ahead in what was seen as quite a humiliating defeat for the community worker, some progressive black women had stood behind the principle of single sex education as such as a separate issue, for reasons which did not run parallel to those of the Muslim Parents' Association. They now had the opportunity to put forward views which accorded at least superficially on this point with the position of the traditionalist Cheetham Hill Muslims. Within the educational working parties and the equal opportunities working parties views were now being put forward, and supported by feminists and the white educational establishment, that girls responded better if taught on their own and that single sex education should therefore be considered as a general principle.

Yet it had already been argued in those terms by the

Cheetham Hill Muslim community; a report from Oxford on sexual harassment and underachievement in schools had been cited. It appeared that a socialist council was able to consider certain views, when articulated as part of a left-wing radical ideology, as bearing on women's development, but was unable to consider the same view when enunciated as part of a religious view. One observer's comment was that 'the local authority was very sensitive to any form of criticism on aspects of their service provision in relation to a multi-racial society. Their policy was by no means sorted out, very much a hotch-potch of issues.' Moreover, a Labour councillor closely involved remarked: 'Fundamentalist religion of whatever kind is suspected quite deeply by progressive people. The motivation behind the pro-gressive single sex movement is seen as liberating, as developing women, but in Muslim terms as repressive, as keeping women in their place.'

For the fundamentalists, part of the problem was that, ideologically suspect within the Labour Party, and unrepresented by the then single black member on the city council, their impact on the council's perception of equal opportunities issues was minimal. Furthermore, the issues had never been argued in the wider context of the appropriateness of educational provision in the city or a multi-racial population. First, the education committee had at the time retreated from a discussion of institutional racism, and the white radicals who ostensibly supported the campaign and might have put forward those arguments were themselves unclear about the extent of their commitment to Muslim demands.

The dilemma for the Cheetham Hill Muslims was that the radical left was prepared to argue for autonomy, even self-determination for black groups, so long as their basic philosophy was compatible with socialist principles as embodied in their manifesto. They themselves would define the norm and the bounds of what was acceptable. Moreover, in the determination of some individuals to pursue their cause from within the democratic system, those barriers would still have to be overcome. In the Gerry Stoker and Tim Brindley study of Leicester city politics, the lack of shared values between white and black councillors was seen as an important factor.

There appears to be a significant gap between the traditional Asian attitudes to family, religion, work and business and the secular and 'progressive' cultural perspective of many Labour councillors and local authority officials.

In a few cases these differences lead to the articulation of more generalised prejudice. This can lead to a view of Asian councillors as unprincipled men on the make. There is suspicion of their supposed business interests and connections and doubts are expressed about the extent of their ideological commitment to socialism. (1985, p. 298)

Marian Fitzgerald notes Labour councillors in a London borough cooling in their enthusiasm for multi-culturalism if it meant funding and giving influence to groups who ran their affairs on non-socialist principles.

There remained concern to involve black people in the party but the desired black involvement became more tightly defined. White party members wanted black, working class socialists and they wanted to be able to weed out those who were only interested in the Labour Party as a vehicle for their own ambition or the promotion of the narrow interests of their particular sub-group. (1984, p. 38)

From 1984, the Labour group in the Manchester City Council turned to the younger black emerging politicians, according to one councillor, increasingly consulting them and giving them more weight than might be expected numerically. Largely based in South Manchester, in areas of young and more mobile multi-racial communities, and building up power bases through youth and community work, they had grown up with the Labour Party, familiar with British and socialist politics, and able to take on a 'more English style of approaching things'. Concentrating on docketing and campaigning on racist incidents and campaigning for improved services, they were able to obtain support from some of the more traditional elements within the community who were dissatisfied with the service departments, or anxious to mobilise the police to deal with racist attacks, as well as appealing to the younger left-wing groups.

Thus the political factor had been a crucial one. Yet the confusion which existed in relation to equal opportunities issues remained unresolved and sometimes unacknowledged. The single sex education issue had suffered from the change in the political complexion of the city council in 1984. The Muslim question was dropped neatly between the dominant right-wing Labour membership of the previous council and their left-wing party colleagues who succeeded them. In the first council, mildly committed to 'good race relations' and with a limited concept and commitment to equal opportunities, the affair was regarded as embarrassing, a political fuss, while the community worker and his white supporters were regarded as on the left of

the party and automatically discredited. For the council which followed, the campaign was regarded as led by male reactionaries and fundamentalists and therefore unacceptable.

The complexity of the outcome matches the complexity of the process. Despite the stronger political position of the younger black politicians and activists, the Manchester Council for Community Relations and the Race Sub-Committee remained dominated by the older element from both north and south Manchester, whose concept of racism centred around the threatened loss of culture and identity. Yet the position of this largely older generation is in many ways an isolated one. They had attempted to bring change from within the system, yet there seemed to be little progress on the major issues at that time: single sex educaton, halal food and Muslim burial. The younger generation from the orthodox group had consistently argued all along that their action should be more strident, even violent. In their distrust of white institutions they had in many ways a common approach with their left-wing counterparts, who identified institutional racism as one of their main targets.

The struggle for resources

If RCP had originally defined its work around a fairly narrow focus, that of urban renewal, it was clear at an early stage that any community development work could not ignore a crucial part of community activity: the conflict between groups for control of resources. That conflict led in three separate but interconnected directions: the struggle for control of the groups themselves; the arena of party political conflict; and into the council's channels of consultation and co-operation – the race relations bodies. As we saw earlier, in such a situation the community worker requires extraordinary skills to avoid accusations of bias.

Marian Fitzgerald quotes Sir George Young's statement: 'There has been an extensive development of ethnic minority organisations who are political with a small "p". The interface with the parties is at the point of bargaining for money.' She continues:

The problem is that this puts the organisations in a very vulnerable position. The immediate gains of funding and the political influence which comes through consultation and co-option may depend on the patronage of one party. If that party loses power groups may be left high and dry and those most closely identified with it may be those

regarded with greatest suspicion by its successor. Moreover, competition for this patronage may divert groups from their primary
purpose and collectively weaken them by intensifying the forces of
division between them. (1984, p. 63)

We have already seen the vulnerability of the RCP worker in
the face of political manoeuvres in the Milkstone Residents'
Association. Later developments in the Castlemere Community
Centre, in many ways the association's creation, demonstrate
how important it is for the worker to take full account of the
political context of community action. Before the CBAA
strategy had localised consultation and influence, Rochdale
Asian politics had centred around the Pakistani Welfare
Association. After the Spotland CBAA office was established in
1979, the welfare association split into two, supported respectively by the Labour and Liberal parties. It was in a desire to
challenge the leadership of the welfare associations and look for
an alternative power base that an ex-shopowner and ex-Labour
councillor had provided much of the initiative and motivation
for the development of the Milkstone Residents' Association in
1982. As early as 1974, when he was a councillor, he had major
differences with the Pakistan Welfare Association in both
approach and personality. By 1983, the residents' association
had become very influential and its Labour chair became the
focus of a power struggle in an area which had been historically
a Liberal one and which returned three Liberal ward councillors.

It is worth recapping the history of the Castlemere Centre.
The original application for an Asian centre in Milkstone had a
chequered and somewhat unclear history, and had involved both
the planning department and the mosque committee. By 1982,
the residents' association had become involved, and what had
been three separate bids for different resources had been
amalgamated into one application following the intervention of
the chief executive who felt the need to make a high profile
input into an area of high Asian population. The empty
Castlemere school was selected as appropriate premises. The
effect of this was to make it a resource of enormous potential
and immense management implications. The community
certainly had an interest in having a building large enough to
hold weddings, but the necessary detailed thinking through of
the management of such a resource was not done at an early
stage.

The fact that the council would always have to take on a

substantial overheads bill had ramifications in terms of how the centre would be managed. Adding to the difficulties was the high profile given to the project by the council which brought the centre into the political sphere at an early date. What was essentially a party political gesture became a focus for political conflict. Council planning department officers had become heavily involved in writing the constitution and a sizeable number of councillors had been written on to the committee. It was therefore seen by political parties as a body to control, and the struggle between black Liberal and Labour Party members followed closely that engaged in by white local politicians.

Various interest groups were reactivated and started to organise, offering primarily an arena for political confrontaton. At stake were places on the executive of Rochdale CRE, control of the residents' association and control of the steering committee for the proposed Castlemere Community Centre. It was the entry of the chairman of the residents' association into mosque politics which finally tipped the balance against his continuing control. By autumn 1983 the Liberals had gained control of the association.

Most of the Liberals were drawn from the younger generation, were articulate and involved in community projects and schemes. Although often unemployed, these young men were in the main supported by borough-wide family links and in that way linked directly into the patronage systems and existing patterns of conflict. However, there was also a new element of inter-generational conflict and this was to find its focus around control of resources.

In this way the community centre had conflict written into its history from the start. When it opened in May 1985, the Liberals gained control and effectively ran the centre until Labour became the majority party on the borough council in 1986. Milkstone politics were inevitably affected by the re-election of the ex-chair of the residents' association to the borough council. By July 1986 two Liberal councillors were removed from the committee and the conflict began. In August 1986, the management of the centre was taken over by the council. This was seen by many observers as not the most obvious or appropriate way of dealing with the issue, and immediately brought about accusations from the MP that it was being done deliberately because the Labour Party wanted control of the committee.

What had happened was that the political patronage previously held solely by the Pakistani Welfare Associations had
widened out. Smaller local community units were now managing tens of thousands of pounds; and the new brokers were
the younger generation who were coming up through the MSC
schemes and the residents' associations. In the 1970s, the
Pakistani Welfare Association had been able to promise local
politicians to deliver a large section of the Asian vote. This had
changed; ward candidates were now in the position of having to
persuade the Asian vote on a variety of issues.

Furthermore, by 1986 the Labour Party was beginning to
explore the power bases within the Asian community previously
monopolised by the Liberals. By 1986 both parties were looking
for ward candidates from within the community. The Bangladeshi
community in Wardleworth, for example, divided internally along
lines of family allegiance and according to village and *thana*, did not
have a history of party political affiliation. However, as the
Bangladesh Association split into two rival groups in 1986, the split
quickly took on a political complexion.

It is possible to see both in Rochdale and Cleveland that the
community development input contributed directly towards this
struggle for resources. Not only were groups using their newly
acquired awareness of the political process for their own purposes, but in many cases community workers were actively
helping groups to draw up applications for major sums of
money. It might be argued that such conflict was the sign of a
new political consciousness in the community and one in which
parallels could be seen in the white community.

However, the manifestations and consequences of this competition for community resources were not all obviously
healthy. Gideon Ben-Tovim points out that funding through
Inner Areas funding is cheap for local governments and can
serve to divert attention away from racial inequalities which are
institutionally generated or maintained through mainstream provision. The failure to link these ad hoc cultural initiatives to any
kind of formal political processes can further serve to protect
local institutions from more fundamental and sustained pressure
from local organisations and groups. (1986, p. 107)

In Rochdale, for example, there are no local government
wards in which the Asian vote could substantially affect electoral
outcomes. Political parties were motivated neither to look for
black candidates nor to take up issues concerning racism and

the needs of the black communities. Indeed such concern was a vote-loser, those councillors who were seen to help their Asian constituents being subject to abuse, encouraged by a local press which fostered popular misconceptions about Asians getting more than their fair share.

However, if this lack of political weight re-emphasises the importance of community-based action, it must also be placed in the context of recent trends in community development. One worker put it this way: first-wave community development in the 1960s promoted analysis of poverty, and steered away from a control of community activity. However, while the second wave of community development uses the same rhetoric of handing over power and teaching people skills, community workers have often got more in common with the agencies that employ them and less to do with the people who live on the estates.

Community workers are professionalised; they are concerned about social issues but it is an extension of service provision. Community development as carried out by MSC workers takes this even further. Workers are not allowed to get into politically contentious issues. Someone who 10 years ago might have been involved in campaigning for a tenants' association on poor repairs will now be going about collecting repairs complaints for the housing department or digging holes to improve the environment. They are now *part of the solution* rather leaving the blame squarely with the providers.

Furthermore, the pressure was on politicians, community leaders and community workers alike to 'deliver the goods', and the business of managing large sums of money and often quite complex schemes was undoubtedly complicated by internal conflict. In Cleveland, the honeymoon period of consultation gave way to a situation of conflict between councillors and community groups. After a little more than a year the enthusiasm for group consultative meetings petered out. The council's credibility suffered a serious blow after opposition to ethnic monitoring, for example, became known. In Rochdale, although there was an expression of support for smaller groups, the logical product of the CBAA process, there would be those who would nevertheless believe that the council continued to have an interest in seeing the community as a bloc in order to underresource it, and that it continued to use factional division as an excuse to withhold local control of resources. Gideon

Ben-Tovim argues precisely this issue:

The question of the point at which participation can mask a process of community management then becomes an important one. The variety of consultative measures in which we have been involved or observed close at hand have served to emphasise the inequalities between consultors and consulted. This has been the case irrespective of the particular form of consultative measure. (1986, p. 101)

Consultative bodies

Competition for funding was also being carried into the new consultative bodies. Gideon Ben-Tovim describes the dangers of this process in more detail:

The parties in this situation become power brokers between black groups; they persist in seeing black people as collectivities, organised into potential power blocs, not as individuals; and, in the name of consultation, they perpetuate the process of mediating 'black opinion' on policy via those 'spokesmen' and 'community leaders' the policy makers recognise. Indeed it is not too fanciful to see some of the present consultative arrangements as an updated, more sophisticated version of the 'race relations' strategies of the 1960s and 1970s – the difference being that whereas previously 'buffer institutions' were created outside the sphere of politics, a 'participatory margin' has now been created within that sphere. This may give those it accommodates the illusion of access to real political influence, yet it may in reality weaken them by creating dependence (on political patronage and, above all, grant aid) and by intensifying inter-group rivalry. (1986, p. 64).

In Cleveland the old CRC was dominated by the Pakistani community and in particular by one individual, to the exclusion, the Indian community felt, of their interests. In 1984 a challenge was successfully put to the CRC by a faction on the grounds that it was unrepresentative and overconcerned with negotiation for resources rather than in taking on an actively campaigning role for improved services. Although a survey issued to all ethnic minority groups on desired methods of consultation had demonstrated a remarkable absence of enthusiasm for the CRC[1], the council did not take up the opportunity of forming an entirely new organisation. County elections were on the horizon and it was politically expedient to leave the issue until after the elections, and too dangerous to appear to discredit or invalidate any one group or faction.

The result was the institutionalisation of the factions, and the formation of a breakaway CRE, more overtly professional in its membership than the old CRC and having openings into the left wing of the party and the formation of a community relations steering committee, with an appointed community relations officer and administrative officer. Conflict centred on the question of confidence in the CRO; in December 1986 a meeting of the Labour members of the council was suspended for 20 minutes following uproar from young left-wing members when two councillors who opposed the CRO were suspended from the steering committee. While the new body received official recognition by the council, not only did the old CRC persist, but it gained representation on the county council's new consultative group for ethnic minorities.

The prospects of this consultative group, established as a sub-group of the equal opportunities sub-committee, looked bleak, given the marginal position of equal opportunities initiatives within the council. As it was, it appeared to many that representatives were more concerned with playing out a power battle within the arena of the consultative group than in challenging council policies in a way which might jeopardise support for their particular faction. The council's proposed extension of consultation into the community was also discouraged for fear that local individual power positions would be further undermined and reduce the effect of support by the council for their faction on the CRC. The council's policy and the pragmatic decisions taken had the effective result both of incorporating community leaders and reinforcing existing leadership patterns within the black community. In contrast to what were seen as positive and sustained initiatives by Middlesbrough Borough Council, who had appointed an equal opportunities officer and were conducting regular neighbourhood consultative meetings, there was a feeling expressed that the mood of the county council had both swung to the right, and there had been a move away from equal opportunities initiatives.

In Rochdale a new type of resident was involved in the process. Before RCP arrived, the council approached the Asian community through the chairmen of the two Pakistani Welfare Associations of Spotland Road and Milkstone Road, which dominated Asian political life. Successful manoeuvres by the Labour-dominated Spotland Road faction to gain control of the

CRE were undermined when an MSC project employing between forty and fifty people was disbanded after accusations by
employees of mismanagement. The new CRC was a combination of the old groups, but it had an important new element:
the men, mainly young, both Labour and Liberal, who had
emerged through the new community groups, for example, the
Kashmir Youth Association and the Bangladesh Community
Project. It was also this new emergent group who were
dominating the council's race relations sub-committee and were
represented on the area committees, the consultative structure
established with residents. Educated in Rochdale, this group
came from a rural Kashmiri background, whereas the old
'leaders' were mainly Punjabis.

With a new chairman, by 1987 the CRC became more influenced by the Labour Party but, looking towards more
campaigning and anti-racist work, there was by no means
agreement with the Labour-controlled council. The old race
relations sub-committee, which had a direct and important link
with personnel, was disbanded in early 1987. A system of
working parties was introduced, of which the black working
party was only one, and which now answered indirectly to
personnel through the equal opportunities committee. The
placing of black issues together with equal opportunities generally was seen as a direct loss of power and to be connected with
less risk-taking generally in relation to anti-racism and to the
fear of a loss of the white vote.

The question of how black groups should be represented in
any consultation process came into focus in Manchester, raising
the difference between racism and other forms of disadvantage.
Until 1984 the council had responded in an ad hoc way to the
demands of groups, without working to any wider strategy. For
example, the education committee started consultation early in
1982 and 1983, talking to community leaders in the mosques
and gurdhwaras. This was a method of consultation which held
little value for those concerned with a broad range of community
issues, who saw discussion restricted by male leaders to religious issues. Not under scrutiny was the use of section 11 as
almost the sole method of employing black professionals in the
city, the nature of parental involvement and levels of racism in
schools, and curriculum issues.

In 1984 the council started from the assumption that all
'disadvantaged' groups felt some common identity and were

prepared to work together to promote equal opportunities issues. An attempt was made to establish an equal opportunities committee which would cover race issues. Unprepared for the negative response from black groups, it took two years for the council to revise its approach and to establish the race committee as a sub-committee of the policy committee with its own staffing unit.

While it may be acknowledged that some interest groups in our areas of study have been able to take advantage of open consultative meetings to debate particular issues, it is rare to encounter any expression of confidence in the council committee structures as a way for small groups to promote their views or interests. Enthusiasm, albeit sometimes guarded for the area committees in Rochdale as a locally-based initiatve and potentially responsive and adaptable, is an exception to this rule.

Local authorities have not penetrated the barriers they have imposed on themselves through inflexibility and bureaucracy. They cannot really know at the end of a desk what are the particular needs of a community or a particular area. Their consultation process is inadequate and their identification of leadership phoney.

This political observer's opinion is that a more realistic approach is the integrated employment of a cross-section of those communities in order to identify needs.

This view may appear to emphasise the importance of the central rather than the local. But it links to a perception which has not seen real local power developed through the medium of existing methods of consultation. Usha Prashar and Sian Nicholas write that the proliferation of sub-committees and working parties also tends to centralise rather than democratise responsibility for policy development. There may be an illusion that consultation is taking place, but it may not necessarily influence policy and practice. Furthermore, consultation does not in itself lead to better service delivery. This depends on respective departments having the determination to modify services and make appropriate service provision in response to the particular circumstances of the black and other ethnic minority communities (1986, p. 48). To this extent any analysis of community action and the bid for participation in the decision-making process would be incomplete without considering the organisational response.

8 Organisational Change and Inter-Agency Work

. . . there exist strong forces within local government which can and have, in our experience, militated against the use of the local public sector as an instrument of positive social change in the pursuit of racial equality. (Gideon Ben-Tovim, 1986, p. 107)

When Cleveland Social Services Department appointed its first neighbourhood worker for ethnic minorities in 1981, it recognised that it lacked both the information and other vital tools required to challenge departmental 'conventional wisdom' on the needs of ethnic minority communities.

Although the next logical step was to provide the structures to receive that information and to re-evaluate services in the light of it, that was not the action taken by the department. Herman Ouseley (1984) describes built-in disadvantages of local authority race relations advisory posts. The characteristics resemble those of many specialist posts created for work with ethnic minority groups. They are:

- grafted on to structures which neither accept that changes in practices are necessary nor that racism exists
- created with the expectation that they will make changes in policy and practices necessary to achieve race equality, yet there is no real understanding by decision-makers of institutional racism, how it operates and what is required in the way of resources, will-power and attitudes to remove it
- established on low grades, with low status, yet they are expected to relate to all levels within the authority

When the third worker took up her post in 1984, she found not only a lack of structures to receive the information, but in their place the working mechanisms of resistance. Where difference between the white and black experience would be explained,

112

there would be an insistance on similarity. She was treated as an expert on the one hand in a way that hindered practitioners from taking on knowledge and information for themselves; on the other hand she felt regarded as a trouble-maker, her views rejected when it suited.

It is often difficult in that situation for a worker, particularly if isolated within a white bureaucracy, to diagnose exactly what is happening. Even when it becomes clear, the worker may feel justifiably daunted by the task of challenging a resistance and tradition-bound system. In Cleveland it was a racism awareness training workshop held in July 1984 which both helped the worker with insight into her own situation, and which provided the promise of a lever with which to promote change.

This coincided with a clarification of her role as a neighbourhood worker. The community house in Granville Road, brought into operation as a base for the Central Middlesbrough Project, had been useful in the development of advice and information work, and emphasis had initially been placed on the development of youth provision in the area through the junior club and the Asian boys' club. However, the experience with groups was not encouraging. An individual approach had proved most productive in work with women and an Asian men's group had been abandoned after a year. The group had been reluctant to introduce any elements of formalisation. Without particular issues on which to focus, it had been found that the less formal benefits of group participation, such as mutual support and personal development, which workers regarded as important in the community development process, were not recognised or valued by the community.

A report on neighbourhood work in Central Middlesbrough in 1983 recognised that there were several reasons why the application of a community development model would be difficult. It suggested that neighbourhood work would be 'issue based' and require co-ordination and liaison with other service agencies. The worker's assessment was that there was a lack of interest in group processes and political awareness from within the community; the probable consequence of effort placed in developing groups would be to strengthen the position of existing community leaders. The community's interest was in obtaining resources; if the group-work model entailed channelling such funding through key figures, it was not seen to promise a structural shift or to place the control of resources with the community.

In some ways the objectives, strategies and day-to-day activies of community-style organisations complement those of the local state extremely well. Some kind of provision is made for the black community and the state can be seen to be playing a supporting role, through for example funding. Rather than challenging institutional provision and practice as a whole, these initiatives sit quite comfortably alongside. (Ben-Tovim *et al.*, 1986, p. 70).

What seemed vital was to provide more jobs and services to black people; in order to do that it would be necessary to challenge the racism within institutions and promote change. To the extent that black people might define their needs in ways which differed from the mainstream, neighbourhood concentration on grass-roots work and the provision of information still appeared valid. However such work should be informed by a political awareness within both the neighbour- hood and the department. Furthermore, it should be reinforced by increased agency resources and the appointment of black key workers as a priority. In Cleveland Social Services black workers were being appointed into an already marginalised sector, that of neighbourhood work. Furthermore, that pattern was being repeated elsewhere in the authority and in other local authorities throughout the country. Black workers were being appointed to liaison officer posts, as interpreters, assistants and to a host of 'specialist' positions. The key general management jobs remained untouched.

It became a priority for the neighbourhood work team to raise awareness of the relevent issues, particularly among the senior officers. The first hurdle for many local authorities in facing such a challenge is the barrier of inertia within departments, particularly when very large proportions of staff have been in post for 10 years or more, one result of a practice of recruitment from within. When this is combined with a lack of management training, it is not surprising to find poor communication, lack of an overall strategy and generally low morale and motivation, the poorest climate for change. Concerns in this situation centre more on maintenance than on objective setting and moving forward, the managers who attempt to implement change regarded as a threat to established order and stability.

Paul Stubbs identifies a debate about the nature of SSDs 'centred on whether social workers are trapped by managerial and hierarchical modes of control or, again, using the concept of relative autonomy, whether there is space for producing changes in the organisation and in the relationships within it in a radical, anti-racist direction'. (1985, p. 7) Herman Ouseley points to the middle managers, senior officers and chief officers as the people key to the process of change. But there is a major obstacle:

They are largely middle class, they have 'made it' in materialistic terms, and they have frequently suburbanised their existence. Not all have lost their empathy with the poor and the deprived, and in fact most will diligently work on behalf of the disadvantaged sections of the community. But because they have moved on and moved away from the problems, many have lost the conviction and determination to be part of the solution. To do so would fundamentally challenge their own position and could result in an erosion of their power and resources. (1984, p. 135)

Within Cleveland County Council the barriers posed by middle management were increased by a distrust for centralised decision making. The county council had been established corporately in the early 1970s, but from an early stage departments had moved away from corporate decision making, following their own line of development. There was considerable opposition to any proposal for an overall management group, and successful resistance by departments such as education and social services to being brought under a central county personnel department. Central strategies for equal opportunities and unemployment were regarded then by some as a dangerous move in the direction of corporate management. Against this background, and with race issues and equal opportunities located within the personnel department, there were in-built difficulties in transferring central initiatives to the service departments.

When the council moved to the right after the 1985 elections the moves against corporate management were strengthened, and the equal opportunities committee lost a degree of support. It was against this background that the neighbourhood work section spearheaded a move within the social services department to establish a working party which had as its remit the development of a departmental equal opportunities strategy in respect of employment and service delivery to ethnic minorities. The 11-point recommendations which emerged included positive action. The department 'accepts its role in combatting racial discrimination through its position as employer, service provider and supporter of the voluntary sector'.[1] The report of the working party was published in September 1985, and the resulting recommendations were adopted as policy by the social services committee in March 1986.

It had not been an easy passage. The seven-month delay in getting the report to committee reflected in large part the blocks put up by middle management. The fundamental challenge had been to gain recognition that racism existed and acceptance that the problem lay within the department, not with the community. It was also recognised that although the neighbourhood team had played a vital part in initiating and facilitating change, there needed to be a more central impetus. As part of the implementation strategy an adviser post for ethnic minorities was established, which would be part of the adviser team within social services, with access to decision making. That post was also to provide the focus for the increasing number of black workers within the department to organise themselves as a self-support group.

There remained major barriers to change. Development of the county's equal opportunities policy remained limited by a lack of enthusiasm. Furthermore, in an absence of corporate planning, social services would have to bid for resources for its change measures against other departmental heads with other priorities and perceptions. Central co-ordination and shared objectives are also crucial in terms of equal opportunities perspectives in recruitment. In Cleveland responsibility for equal opportunities lay with a disintegrating personnel department; social services, operating its own personnel section, did not see it as part of its remit to get involved in equal opportunities, and had not developed its own policy. Without a thorough understanding of how recruitment procedures and personnel specifications for all staff should reflect changed priorities, there will inevitably be a mismatch between changing strategies and newly-appointed personnel.

There was another inconsistency. Decentralisation theoretically located services within the neighbourhood but, operating from a pre-existing case-work structure, denied neighbourhood workers any real influence within management structures. Ironically, then, it was difficult for grass-roots neighbourhood work to effect decision making at a district level, increasing a tendency towards change being directed from the centre. The result was a diminished social-planning role for neighbourhood workers and a major gap between central decision making and district management.

Inter-agency work

One of the prime elements of the Cleveland neighbourhood workers' job description was 'developing and maintaining relationships with other departments of the county council, the borough councils and other agencies often acting in a liaison capacity'. Such inter-agency work was designed primarily to increase awareness amongst other agencies, both statutory and voluntary, of community needs, leading to greater sensitivity on the part of those agencies when considering the provision of service. It was seen as a component of the worker's duties, then, to develop inter-agency meetings and personal contact between the worker and the agencies, and to give advice, information or co-operation in the development of specific projects.

The Central Middlesbrough Project was an inter-agency group convened by the first Cleveland neighbourhood worker for ethnic minorities early in 1981. Initially the focus of the group was on matters relating directly to black communities in Central Middlesbrough, a brief later widened out to take in issues affecting the Central Middlesbrough community as a whole. Group membership was drawn from professionals in the project area, and its objectives were initially at the level of liaison between agencies, exchange of information on existing service provision, and on the relationship between black and white communities in Middlesbrough. There was also an explicit objective to act as an influencing group, encouraging policy change and formulation.

In the early meetings there was a strongly felt need for greater general education of white workers on the nature of Islam and information on the area of Pakistan from which people came. However, this led swiftly to an awareness of racism, reflecting a more general contemporary change in attitudes and approach. A representative from the Centre for Multi-Cultural Education, for example, records that over the period the centre's general objectives shifted gradually from simply attempting to provide for the linguistic and cultural needs of black communities towards a policy of multi-cultural and anti-racist education for all.

A school liaison officer, who had attended meetings since the early days, saw a major change in attitudes in schools, which had started in the late 1970s. There was a recognition of the need to understand parents' expectations from the educational system, and more generally to open up dialogue with parents through individual contact, and the overcoming of possible language barriers. School books have been examined for racism and the use of first languages in the classroom has been aided by the appointment of bilingual teaching auxiliaries.

However, the experience of the Middlesbrough Project Group does point up some of the limitations to such a self-education programme in promoting a 'bottom-up' change. Even within single departments, the 'knock-on' effect is often limited. Within schools, for example, change depended very much on the commitment of an individual head teacher. Change was organic and haphazard as teachers moved between schools, rather than co-ordinated and directed. Although individuals were often able to take back discussion to their agency, there were seldom formal report-back systems. The effect of individuals was often only indirect; most individuals would see the project group as having little impact at the level of policy formation. One of the difficulties in attempting to bring about changes in awareness education, for example, was the 'great number of current issues in education competing for the attention of heads and teachers'. Moreover, head teachers were unable to see their personal attendance at discussion meetings such as that of the project group as cost-effective, or as a priority, even if support were given to other staff to attend.

Members of the group were aware that they probably needed to monitor their work, to gather facts and figures, if they were to discover whether their service had been provided in a sensitive and appropriate manner. What was happening was a lengthy process of isolated changes taking place within the system, with the missing link remaining that of policy co-ordination from the top. For example, the involvement of an officer of the education department in the project group led to the development of a racism awareness training programme within the education department, which was extended to teachers on a voluntary basis. Although it was felt that it would be valuable to share the programme inter-departmentally, separate departmental finances dictated that it remain limited to education department staff.

The strategic barriers to change present in the local authority departments are not found to the same degree in a smaller non-statutory agency, although there may well be other obstacles as important. A Middlesbrough Citizens Advice Bureau representative attended the project group from its first meetings, with the back-up of the bureau management committee and a pre-existing awareness of the need for better service provision as a whole. Furthermore, in parallel, CAB nationally was aware that it needed to look closely at its provision for ethnic minorities. The information produced by the National Association of Citizens Advice Bureaux was improved, including an anti-racist statement and discussion and guidance papers.

There was an early acceptance that the Middlesbrough CAB was not providing a service to the Asian community. As a result, in February 1983, as part of the bureau's neighbourhood advice scheme, an outreach worker was established at Granville Road Community House, where about a third of the callers each month were black. This had only limited success, and the Asian Advice Project was launched under the Community Programme, with two black workers with appropriate language skills. It is felt that this project and the employment of some Asian volunteers greatly improved the general quality of service delivery, although the evident drawback of CP funding was that well-trained advice workers had to leave and be replaced after a year, one worker resigning after six months.

We have noted elsewhere the continued importance of advice and information provision in Middlesbrough, given the high level of unemployment in black groups and dependence on state benefits. The Central Middlesbrough neighbourhood worker worked with the welfare rights service to develop a project to raise an awareness of benefits in the ethnic minorities, and with another advice agency, the Marriage Guidance Council, who became aware of how ill-equipped they were to deal with Asian clients. Work was also done with health education officers to develop multi-lingual resources, aimed at women in particular, and to develop information relating to dietary habits and customs for health visitors.

One of the real difficulties for the project was its maintenance of a sense of purpose over the years, and there was a loss of key agencies and individuals. Certainly the functioning of the project as a discussion group was found less successful over time. As new people joined, it sometimes felt to other participants that they were covering old ground, and that they needed to meet new needs. There was an unresolved discussion, for example, as to whether they should operate as a pressure and campaigning group.

The role of the neighbourhood worker in the development of the project group as secretary and chair, providing a focus for inter-agency liaison was a relatively clear one. However, the co-operation and liaison role is less so, the perception by agencies and workers often conflicting. Successive workers saw agencies that did not send representatives to the project group remaining unable to make substantial moves towards an appropriate service, and continuing to call on the neighbourhood workers for skills such as translation. This was professionally unsound and the workers felt such agencies were aware that they had a problem, but 'were expecting the workers to make changes for them'.

Paul Hoggett (1984, p. 20) quotes P. Dunleavy's description of 'policy communities' which exercise hegemony over the relevant areas of professional production. The worker's product is influenced not so much by central or local government, but by the relevant professional community itself, a community that consists not only of sections of local government and service personnel, but of training institutions and related professional bodies. Management control, relating to staff conduct, day-to-day decisions and the making and monitoring of performances in the light of standards set is vital and it is this operational control which is of enormous importance to consumers because it has a decisive impact on the *quality* of service.

It is this control, then, which must be the concern of community action. Just such a role as that performed by the Central Middlesbrough Project Group is a vital one, ideally bringing together 'bottom-up' change and linking it precisely to those policy communities. For the level of change implicated, neighbourhood work went beyond collecting information and representing the views of the community to the officers of the borough and county councils and other agencies responsible for implementing change at a long-term planning level: it meant challenging assumptions. Moreover, such liaison could not replace dialogue with consumers of services. And, without a clarification of the role of the centre, of local government policy in its movement towards race equality, and without guidance in terms of implementation and resource allocation through departments, movement towards change would inevitably be a slow and haphazard affair.

9 Outcomes, Models and Methods

Community resources

What, in its interaction with other processes, has community development achieved in our areas of study? Given the broad interpretation that can be given to the most widely accepted community work aims of changing power structures and resource distribution, and shared knowledge and information through collective action, our example of RCP possibly offers a clear focus in its objective of increased resident 'participation' and decision making in urban renewal. In terms of tangible benefits to the community, one starting point would be to look for changes in the physical environment. At the same time this should throw light on whether there had been any real transfer of power and decision making to communities.

In *Design for Living* the two workers in Sparthbottoms wrote their account of the building of the Sparth Community Centre, of the transformation of an area of urban blight to one which was regarded widely as a model for environmental improvement:

Sparthbottoms is now a pleasant place to walk round on a nice day. The work of urban renewal is virtually complete. Only a few pockets of wasteland, and a few derelict houses, remain to be attended to. The central area, previously a swamp in winter, has been drained, supplied with benches and planted with trees, and a footpath has been laid across to the bridge over the river. The L-shaped community centre stands in one corner, tucked in between an all-weather games pitch and the smart new row of bungalows for old people, as a visible testimony to what residents' associations can achieve.
(Mohammed Habeebullah, 1986, pp. 12–13)

There were visually dramatic changes in other Rochdale wards. The Milkstone CBAA began in August 1978. By 1986 the area had undergone a process which included demolition, rehabilitation and new-build housing through St Vincent's Housing Association, the take-up of improvement grants by individual households and blocks of houses and the use of 'face-lift' money for other environmental improvements. In many streets nearly all the houses had been improved with grants and some terraces were given a new external appearance following the 'enveloping' programme of 1983/84. In some cases, where individual improvements to houses was too expensive, block improvement schemes had been carried out, whereby all the houses were improved together. In 1985/86, a 'face-lift' scheme along the Milkstone Road improved the appearance of a number of shops. New traffic schemes were introduced following consultation with residents, streets and rear alleys resurfaced, and in many cases following house demolition, play areas were opened and garden extensions built for houses which previously had only a small back yard.

The increased confidence developed by the resident involvement in the CBAA programme in those areas was paralleled and indeed affected by the vital role played by residents in the development of community amenities in their neighbourhoods. The Sparth Community Centre was built to a design worked out by the community's own architect, and balanced the needs of white and Asian residents through details such as the provision for a room for religious and language instruction with a separate entrance at one end of the building, and a large hall with a bar at the other, and a kitchen with an industrial cooker to cater for weddings and other ceremonies. Residents had achieved a responsiveness to needs not usually found in the standard design to which council architects worked.

The centre opened in March 1985 with an independent and multi-racial committee which, encouraged by the warden, was gradually able to take on a more confident approach. Starting with mother-tongue teaching and a youth club, within two years the centre was being used by cookery classes, a girls' sewing group, a playgroup, dance and keep-fit class and separate English classes for women and men. In October 1986, the employment of two Asian outreach workers, an assistant community worker and a sports co-ordinator under MSC funding considerably altered the role of both the management committee and the warden. The constitution was changed to represent user groups as well as resident representatives, reflecting the maturing of those groups as many of them become more structured and developed their own management committees and access to funding. The immediate possibilities for self-management by Asian women remained limited by social constraints; although Asian women were involved in the playgroup, for example, in 1987 the committee contained seven black resident representatives, but three white women representing user groups. However, there was change: barriers were breaking down, and women were acquiring confidence and attending social mixed gatherings for the first time.

The wardens of the community centres in both Sparthbottoms and Wardleworth would see development as necessarily a slow one. At the Wardleworth Centre there were changes from the early days when Asian boys only attended the mother and toddler groups; there can, the warden feels, be no sudden transition to management control by the mothers. However, she believes that a multi-racial centre in itself encourages the involvement of Asian women because of the general context of women's activities. In 1986 the Muslim Women's Association was started in Wardleworth and was represented on the centre management committee.

There were other qualitative changes. Both the senior citizens and the youth group changed from being white groups to being racially mixed, the senior citizens introducing formal discussions on social issues and aspects of customs and cultures. The involvement of residents in housing issues through the CBAA had at the same time stimulated an awareness of the possible channels of access to council service departments. While the debate continued as to whether the planning department would hand over employment responsibilities to the management committee, when the CBAA closed in 1986 people were ready to look outwards from the centre to other issues. There was both a new awareness of racism and discussion of strategies to combat its manifestations.

For both areas the community centres represented changes less visible than that evident in bricks and mortar improvement. In 1981, the communities in Sparth were described in *Design for Living* in the following way:

It would be difficult to think of two groups with less in common than a population of long-established, ageing and to some extent demoralised working class Lancastrians (including many of Irish Catholic ancestry) and a population of non-English speaking Muslim immigrants from rural backgrounds. Though Sparthbottoms has been happily free of the grosser manifestations of racism such as assaults on individuals and their property, it was almost inevitable that the two groups should have become divided by ignorance, suspicion and mutually antagonistic stereotypes. While a number of white residents blamed Pakistanis for the physical decline of the neighbourhood, a number of Pakistanis shunned closer contact with whites for fear that social integration could lead to their children being contaminated by the 'depraved' values of a permissive society. (Mohammed Habeebullah, 1986, pp. 4 & 5)

The struggle for the development of a community centre and resident negotiations with the council on improvement policy led to a new respect for each other's culture and way of life.

In Wardleworth in 1981 the community had been divided not only along the lines of black and white populations, but by antagonism between Pakistanis and Bangladeshis. Further, within the Pakistani population the conflict between those from the minority Mirpuri population and the largely urban-based Punjabis was a vital element in Pakistani political and social life, surfacing in a highly volatile way in mosque politics, for example. Over and above this was tribal rivalry, and these conflicts were exploited by and fed into party politics.

In the half decade which followed there was a changed sense of community in the area in very real ways. Despite the party politicisation of the conflict and divisions outlined above, at the level of local action the various communities came together and saw the benefit of working in a group, even though at times individual group interests continued to predominate. One of the advantages of having a multi-racial centre was that means had to be found to accommodate the competing demands and needs for resources. The CBAA structure also enabled a mobilisation of support across communities, for example in negotiating over the council's proposal to spend £70,000 on a new play area. On another occasion, when the Labour Party's manifesto proposed new-build housing in an area previously earmarked for a mosque, councillors were lobbied, and the Muslim case was presented successfully by the area committee representing the community as a whole.

Thus in Wardleworth, as indeed in other wards, there was street-level pressure, CBAA and later area committee activity, joint management by user groups of the community centre and thriving community projects such as the Bangladesh Project and the Kashmir Youth Project. It is difficult to assess how much each of these factors contributed to the new sense of sharing and distribution of power.

Whatever the impact of multi-racial centres locally, their success must be seen alongside the development of black projects; these strengthened and reinforced local multi-racial activity. The Castlemere Centre in Milkstone ran a girls' club, English and Arabic classes, a mother and toddler group, an Age Concern group, and a youth worker was employed with MSC funding to run library and youth activities. The centre had a large kitchen fully equipped for Asian cooking with a large hall and adjoining smaller rooms suitable for holding wedding ceremonies. In many respects it was seen as an all-Rochdale Asian facility. Yet its difficulties highlighted the political, funding and management problems presented by so large a resource. Therefore one of the crucial factors to emerge, the exploitative edge to the relationship between party politicians and their black constituents, focused on and found expression in resource provision.

One of the operational difficulties of the Castlemere Centre was finding the revenue funding for the proposed computer and motor mechanics workshops, capital funded by the original project proposal. Training needs within the Asian community and an ability to respond to those needs within the community itself had been demonstrated effectively by the Kashmir Youth Project. A KYP survey had indicated that although Asian young people were expressing needs and motivation for training, they were not getting on to courses, such as those provided by Rochdale's Training Centre at State Mill, or they were leaving them with their training incomplete. The project had responded by designating training provision as a priority. Workshops were set up for sewing, motor mechanics, and television and video repairs. The sewing workshop was the first on its feet, many of the trainees afterwards obtaining jobs. The level of training in television repairs and motor mechanics would not equip trainees for immediate employment; what was seen as important was breaking down their own and other people's preconceptions about aptitude and motivation. Related to this, the project responded to complaints by the community that Asian young people were not benefiting from YTS by organising a seminar attended by 25 companies.

Employment seminars were also held to which councillors, council officers, and the race relations adviser were invited. The project was able to have a demonstrable effect on the council's employment policies; following the change in requirements for formal 'O' and 'A' level results, there was an opening up of local authority recruitment.

In Rochdale in 1987 a survey carried out by the CRE showed that of 16,000 Asians living in Rochdale, unemployment was at over 60 per cent, three times greater than the unemployment rate of the whole town; they suffered drastically and disproportionately from the recession in the local textile trades. Of those in employment, 37 per cent were self-employed. In response to questions about their knowledge of assistance, such as the wages subsidy scheme, young workers' scheme, capital grants, and enterprise allowance scheme, the majority in this group had no knowledge of, nor experience in, making applications for this assistance. Nor were Asian businessmen supported by groups such as the chamber of commerce or the chamber of trade.

The RCP worker in the Milkstone area felt that small businesses and employment creation were a legitimate area of activity. The old traders' asociation in Milkstone was re-formed and put pressure on the council to spend 'face-lifting' money on improving a block of shops in the Milkstone Road planned for demolition. Following a meeting of businessmen, applications were put forward for Inner Areas funds; grants were obtained to refurbish existing buildings and for machinery, creating new jobs in clothing and other small manufacturing enterprises.

At the time there was little support from RCP as such, most team members feeling restricted within the narrow guidelines of the project. However, by 1985 a clear view was established that rapidly rising unemployment levels were at the root of many of the problems of poverty and deprivation in Rochdale, and that the project could develop assistance in that area. The project put forward an unsuccessful Inner Areas bid for a co-operative and community development unit which would assist with the development of co-operatives and community businesses.

Yet it is these projects which appear to offer the most tangible benefits of community development which require further examination. In Rochdale the workers at KYP, the Bangladesh project, some of the workers at Sparth and most of the workers at Castlemere were all MSC funded, and as such subject to all the disadvantages of low wage scales and temporary employment. Capital funding was also external, often from a variety of sources. One council officer comments:

The problem is that we are so dependent on external funding that the packages we buy are not always the most appropriate for the whole of Rochdale or even for any particular section you are looking at. You go to the EEC and there is a particular amount of funding for project of type X and if you want the funds you go for type X and there you are into a tight framework of auditors and accountability.

There is a real problem for local authorities in terms of taking on such funding into mainstream budgets, particularly when there may already be a substantial shortfall, in, for example, maintaining community buildings. First, there is the danger that if additional funds are raised through the rates the council will be liable to central government penalties. And in a local authority such as Manchester, the political dissociation from CP schemes results in a lack of support and monitoring of such schemes and even less likelihood of moving such projects into the mainstream.

KYP might well feel confident that it had demonstrated and responded to needs so dramatically that its future would remain safeguarded whatever funding crisis it might encounter. Yet the operation of the project still suffered from the nature of MSC funding itself. It was unable to respond to employment needs within the community; the requirement to find someone who had not been even in part-time employment meant that workers were often recruited from outside Rochdale. It was also difficult to employ local Asian women, many of whom, although unemployed, were not registered or in receipt of benefit.

The short-term employment and turnover of personnel inherent in CP staffing also meant that there was a skills loss, not just to the project and the local community, but on a wider scale to Rochdale. The project's far-reaching reputation meant that many ex-employees found employment in neighbouring towns. Skills present within the project were also deflected into applications for funding extension and the search for new staff, in a response to the MSC's bureaucratic requirements. This was energy which could have been put into community development and into pressure on council services.

There were evident benefits from these projects. Success brought confidence. Companies and training schemes started looking for Asian applicants. There was also a general opening up of channels of communication between the service departments and the communities. Both KYP and the Bangladesh Project have a formal advice-giving element which provides liaison, and each project has representatives of local authority departments on their management committees. Project members would not suggest that changes in service provision have been radical, but would point to the turnabout in attitude of the education department, in their opening up of school buildings to community activities after school hours. For KYP it seemed an important point of recognition when the chief education officer wrote to all schools asking them to give access to KYP for careers advice.

Power sharing

Leadership poses a problem for community workers. They cannot themselves act as leaders and where traditional élites are reactionary and unresponsive, they cannot develop their programmes around existing leadership roles. Nor can they appoint alternative leaders since those should emerge naturally. They are, however, trained to deal with the problems of leadership and have various tactics at their disposal. They may succeed in isolating reactionary elements or persuade them to abide by the wishes of the majority. They may also be able to integrate both traditional and emergent leaders in the new decision-making bodies and in this way, build a coalition of interests that unites the different factions. (Midgely, 1986, p.113)

If in Rochdale there was not such a coalition, there was at least a new accommodation of interests and a freeing up of access to power within communities. RCP was one of a number of factors which acted on the community to bring about such change. Many of those who came to sit on the new area committees had come up through organisations with which RCP was involved. In 1988, for example, a Sparth Asian Association member was not only chair of the Sparth Community Centre Management Committee, but of the borough's race working party. Groups had certainly developed a more sophisticated view of how the council functioned. Previously there had been attempts to influence a single individual perceived as influential. This style was developed by the Pakistan Welfare Association which had originally been established by a Kashmiri when dealing with the income tax and the passport offices. When he left Rochdale in the early 1970s that platform was taken over by professionals from among the East Africans and Pakistanis from Lahore, who had also established themselves as mosque trustees. The welfare associations had shielded people from the realisation that it was possible to extend the boundaries of the system which controlled decision making, and indeed to break into it.

The Kashmiri community was a closely-knit one, Rochdale neighbours often coming from neighbouring villages in Mirpur. By the late 1970s it was their children, Rochdale educated, who were to provide a challenge to the Punjabi and East African Asians who had previously dominated the community. The idea of starting a young people's organisation originated in 1979. Although one of the early founders was on the mosque committee and well placed in the community, most of those involved were not professionals, but employed in factories or as taxi drivers.

KYP originally registered as a youth club. What remained striking in its development was the continuing energy provided by its youthful membership. The project remained open and dynamic, its constitution designed to prevent the management committee from becoming stagnant, and having an upper age limit to membership of 35 years. It canvassed fresh membership through publicity and leafleting, and had a ready entry point through youth clubs and schools.

The Punjabi leadership had been reinforced through its association with the political parties in Rochdale, much of its political influence within the community coming from its links with councillors and the local MP. To some extent a lack of political affiliation by KYP operated to its advantage, as its members adopted more wide-ranging lobbying techniques. When one of the KYP members did put forward his candidacy at the local elections, he met with heavy opposition from the older generation. The feeling was, he says, 'that the young people have taken the community from us. Now they are taking the political parties from us'. Yet the welfare associations, albeit with a lower profile, continued to function, in part because political parties wanted them, although they have lost their welfare rights role. What is ended is the exclusivity of leadership. The CRC had also been run in the past by professionals; by 1986 there were ex-mill workers on the executive, some of whom had come up through the Bangladesh Project and the Sparth Community Centre.

Those active in KYP accept that they too might be regarded within the community as leaders, but see important differences:

What we try to do is to see the community's need first and then find a ground to stand on and take the community forward. The first generation haven't played any role as to long-term problems. They would rather give a comment on certain political things happening in Pakistan or Rochdale, whereas we don't see it as worthwhile to pass comments on situations and then stay at home.

From a community perspective then, funding for projects had enabled people to come together within centres around concrete activities and issues and the CBAA programme itself had provided concrete tasks and issues around which people could develop enthusiasms. This in turn developed forms of organisation and a cultural expression which went beyond religious and traditional social activities, and was rooted within the realities of urban British life.

From an institutional point of view there would appear to be changes. In the 1970s the council had perceived the community in terms of control. By the mid-1980s this was no longer operable. Council officers were responding to a greater number of individuals and groups. As one officer puts it, 'I don't think the council would have been aware of people lobbying for a sports club 15 years ago.'

However, one must treat with caution conclusions about qualitative differences in the relationship between the local authority and communities. One individual involved in KYP would insist that the transfer of resources itself is more apparent than real. KYP neither had control of its premises, nor of its capital grants, funds often being paid out to council architects and contractors. The lease arrangements for the project's premises, an old printing works, were made and controlled, not by KYP, but by the council, and the design of the building itself was heavily influenced by council officers. Furthermore, the politicians, he argues, are still addressing themselves to a white audience.

They say: 'We have given you this centre.' But who have they given it to? We, the Rochdalians, and look how we had to fight for it. And the way those people talk about it sounds as if the Asians are being given a special treat. But all that money is going back to the council.

External money had been brought in under the community's name, but, he feels, the real recipients were the borough council. 'We have been used and we know it.'

Reflecting on greater resident control, he says he feels 'not very optimistic'. One councillor's view would accord with this.

You can bring people together, but in terms of preventing Asian people being shoved out of the community-based action areas, no, it still goes on. We are nowhere near understanding the process of how it happens. If you improve the quality of housing in an area you can bet that the percentage of Asians in that area will drop.

We do not have statistics which would substantiate this view, and it is not an impression which is wholly shared by RCP workers.

Frustration is also expressed about 'shared decision-making'. The Rochdale Metropolitan Community Development Corporation, for example, which was set up to look at council funding under the Inner Areas Programme, found that its own list of priorities carried no weight against that of the council officers' working party. There is also strongly voiced comment about the inability of projects to ignore political influence or pressure, often directly through the presence of councillors and officers on management committees, and the ultimate sanction being the loss of funding or management control.

The obvious example in Rochdale is provided by the history of the Castlemere Centre. Invested with importance from the start by council officers and politicians, the Liberals gained early control of the management committee. Conflict came to a head with accusations of financial mismanagement. The council intervened, creating a new structure whereby they had direct management control. The very fact of political polarisation, the almost adversarial nature of local politics, militated against handing over to local control. Management committees of neighbourhood groups required training and support rather than control, but the council was unable or unwilling to release funds for that purpose. To a certain extent community development provided on-the-spot training, but since both community workers and committee members move on, skills are lost. Without such skills, neighbourhood control is ephemeral, and indeed lack of those skills can be used by the local authority, as in the case of the Wardleworth Centre, as an argument against handing over employer and other responsibilities to management committees.

James Midgely argues that if state sponsorship of community participation neutralises authentic participation, it may be necessary to accept a more limited definition. This recognises the difficulties of achieving absolute popular control over local affairs and the total involvement of all members of the community, concentrating rather on obtaining maximum resources and services from agencies in order to improve social conditions. There may be a need to recognise that there is no real 'bottom-up' development so long as there is an external agent. (1986, p. 151)

If there were grave limitations in terms of project initiatives, how far then could area committees be seen as an exercise in power-sharing? Attendance at committees varied between areas. When there are real issues for debate, such as the relative merits of enveloping as against block improvement schemes, attendance is high. In other areas, high levels of community participation peaked in previous years. In Milkstone, for example, as most of the issues in the CBAA were resolved and it closed down, levels of activity dropped. Area committees were established at the same time as this downturn in activity; representatives on the area committee were the rump of the activists, but the organisations to which they were accountable were in decline. However, the very differences between committees was seen as evidence of their community-based nature, the process cyclical rather than one of continuous development. Even where community activity dies down, the difference from the early days is that 'if necessary, representatives can call the community together again. The lessons they learnt from community activity are there.'

There are distinct limitations. Residents have little power when faced with a compulsory purchase order, are often distanced from technical assistance by jargon, or unwilling to use the design agency which is on offer. However, one councillor puts an alternative view. For the first time residents were being offered the same professional input as the councillors, so that the limits to their decision-making power were similar.

Once there is an attempt to put what power as the council has out to different areas, one thing residents realise is how much less power the council has than they thought. A lot of that power is linked to a question of resources. With professional input into such areas as traffic management and play policy, people can have real options. When it comes to central government funding affecting improvement grants there are limits; the local council as well as residents are ultimately dependent on the Department of the Environment and other government departments.

Organisational change and racism

If we are seeking to examine the development of community groups, the question must equally be asked how far agencies have themselves learnt and changed. What has been vividly demonstrated is that there are contradictions inherent in working with black communities when equal opportunities are absent from the structure of the agency itself, and when there is a failure to come to grips with racism at the stage of project design. Only too frequently agencies perceive equal opportunities in terms of a focus on black communities rather than on their own ethos, structures and functioning.

In Rochdale, despite consultation procedures, there was a feeling that little had changed in terms of council services as appropriate to multi-racial neighbourhoods. As in Cleveland, Rochdale Council was not well-organised in any corporate sense. Officers were constrained within departmental spheres of influence. There was no 'up-front' discussion about appropriate services, and the amount of research and analysis carried out was not consistent with any serious or special attention to community needs.

Contributing to this inability to seize the issue was an adverse popular reaction to perceived developments in the Asian community, encouraged by the tone of the local press. There was a strong backlash to the amount of Inner Areas funding going to Asian groups from within the council itself, to the degree that agencies were being warned against encouraging further bids from Asian groups. There was a continued fear by politicians of the response of the white community, a political response to the enormous increase in racism which accompanied increased levels of unemployment.

A pertinent question is whether RCP would have been more effective in its own comments to the council about employing more black people if the project itself had been seen to be employing people from within the community. Moreover, despite pressure from Rochdale Voluntary Action to rethink the management style of the project as it entered its second phase, discussion on the issue was not followed through with substantial changes. The priority remained that of establishing links with the council rather than community accountability or participation in management of the project. CPF would argue that nationally it is now clearer about its identity and experience as a white-managed organisation, and there is thinking about ways to move forward, including the implications of working in multi-racial areas and with multi-racial teams. However, at least one of the RCP workers would insist that there are lessons which are not being learnt. The issue is not only how far agencies learn about working with black communities, but how far they allow those perceptions to alter more general approaches about appropriate organisational structures and general work practice in a multi-racial society. The two are fundamentally related.

In the inter-agency work in Cleveland one of the important factors was the extent to which change remained vested in individuals, or transmitted to the organisation itself. Community development must affect 'top down' policy direction in order to achieve effective change without losing its grass-roots contact; it is a difficult balancing act.

In Cleveland Social Services Department a major shift was required for the basic recognition that discrimination did take place at the level of departmental services, but there still remained questions as to whether the prevailing organisation norms which ultimately dictated policy development could be touched. Some of the consequences of the lengthy process of debate was the introduction of trained interpreters and the establishment of an Asian Enquiry Line. By 1987, Cleveland SSD had established certain posts for specific work with ethnic minorities: an adviser with responsibility for 'the development and implementation of county council and departmental policies concerned with ethnic minorities', a welfare rights officer with Punjabi and Urdu language skills, a neighbourhood worker, social worker and clerk with language skills.

Additionally, five social work visitor posts with language skills in Urdu, Punjabi, Bengali and Chinese were agreed under mainstream funding. Other posts in the package put forward in March 1987 were to be funded under section 11. These were two under-fives development officers and two welfare rights officers with language skills, a training officer post in racial equality and a research and monitoring post relating to the department's provision for ethnic minorities and the county council's equal opportunities policy. Peter Ferns, writing about such initiatives in SSDs, warns: 'Creating new posts gives the impression that something is being done about racism, and this can be further enhanced if the posts are filled by black people . . . Many of these so-called ethnic minority posts are reduced to advisory roles and monitoring functions, without any power to implement change.' (1987)

Clearly the position of the neighbourhood worker was a marginalised one in relation to decision-making. If there was some progress in Central Middlesbrough in the first half of 1980s in terms of working with black communities, this progress was not being made elsewhere. The neighbourhood section's social profile of North Thornaby written in 1987 mirrored exactly that of Central Middlesbrough half a decade previously. Local Asians did not recognise or identify with the services offered through the three community centres. Despite the very large proportion of Asians in the under-15 age group, Asian teenagers were not using any of the centres, and very few Asian parents were using the under-fives facilities. Despite the SSD's declared commitment to positive action following the working party report on service delivery to ethnic minorities, 'unfortunately there is little indication that services are being tailored to this policy and this is largely a problem of implementation'. The worker responsible for the report felt that progress in health visitors and in schools was not echoed in social services. There were other priorities for the department, and initiatives were left at an individual level. Yet attitudes were a major barrier to implementation and 'make it very difficult in getting on with the job'. The position of the ethnic minorities adviser made it possible to push for some of the accepted changes, but she feels cynical about the strength of her position without the framework of corporate planning or a strategic approach to equal opportunities and anti-racism; responsibility for change, she feels, has been placed with her rather than with managers.

In Cleveland, despite consultation procedures, there has been little change in the relationship of communities to power and resources. Groups have more information, and there is not the same reluctance to take up services. Although the Central Middlesbrough worker's involvement with groups such as the boys' club and the girls' class concentrated on movement towards self-management and greater involvement in community initiatives, young people were largely excluded from higher profile initiatives. These were less concerned with pressure for self-management than with a continuing struggle for the basics: collectively, a concern for independent premises for religious and social organisation, and individually, for survival in the context of increasing economic pressure. The International Centre, which opened in March 1986, and which provided office space for nine or ten different communities, was in many ways the expression of hopes deceived. The Pakistani community had originally been promised a centre of their own, and for them and other communities, the fight for an independent community centre remained the focus of community action. Meanwhile, the Granville Road Community House continued to be used by some of the smaller communities in Central Middlesbrough, the Yemenis, the Somalis and Vietnamese.

What is striking in the Middlesbrough project is the continued emphasis on the provision of advice and information, a function contained within job descriptions. For the Central Middlesbrough worker this was formalised into a once weekly advice and information session. Also based at Granville Road were two part-time advice workers, one Yememi and one Somali. Additionally the CAB held two sessions, providing a service in Urdu, Punjabi and Hindi. In writing about the Yemeni and Somali project, the department expressed its perception of its advice relationship with black communities:

One factor that differentiates this project from other advice sessions is that the nature of the service is sensitive to the particular language barriers experienced by these communities, in that adequate communication involves not only the understanding of spoken and written languages, but a comprehension of a person's cultural baseline and perspective.

Yet this takes the community development worker on to dangerous ground: there is a point at which the worker loses professional identity. One of the black workers in the neighbourhood team in 1987 was taking up a psychology and counselling course because, although 'there is no way a white worker would be expected to do it', she feels that she is expected to offer a counselling service. Yet the council had a substantial welfare rights service, and in 1987 the social services started its own telephone Asian Advice Line. The experience of workers in Rochdale and Manchester has been that, having started with an advice role, it has been possible to build up structures enabling them to move on to group organisation and concentration on tasks and issues. This had not proved possible in Cleveland. Further, given that with changes in MSC regulations many agencies will no longer be able to provide advice services through Community

Programme workers, the likelihood is that Cleveland neighbourhood workers will be no further from escaping from the advice role.

One determining factor would appear to be the general context of availability of resources within the community. In Manchester, as well as a separate welfare rights section, there has been funding for neighbourhood advice centres, whereas in Middlesbrough the funding to the non-statutory sector is extremely limited. The concept of community development must be structured and constrained by its environment. Neighbourhood work operated in the context of an essentially paternalistic local authority. The local authority had a tradition of providing for, rather than working with the community. The authority's concept of community development offered no challenge to this. For the worker, to those constraints was added those of a community without a resource level on which to build; those support structures which could be assumed for white communities were not there for black people. As Ranjit Sondhi points out, racism magnified with Asian communities all the processes connected with working class communities in decay. (1982)

In Manchester there was a more evident move towards positive action. When the left took control in 1984 there was a commitment to unfreezing posts which had previously been left vacant. The resultant expansion through both mainstream and section 11 funding resulted in a virtual tripling of staff levels in the community development section. By 1987, about a quarter of these posts were held by black workers, some 50 per cent with section 11 funding.

In terms of projects on the ground, MSC funding assisted a blossoming of community activity. Longsight in south Manchester, for example, where once there had been only the women's refuge and a girls' youth club, saw the emergence of a Bangladeshi project, and a Pakistani community centre, established with similar objectives to the Rochdale Centres, to provide a venue for wedding functions, but which also developed women's and under-fives issues. But if MSC funding assisted community activity in some cases, it often carried with it, as we have seen elsewhere, a built-in failure component. The unsatisfactory nature of the funding resulted in the collapse of the Asian Project which provided resources for disabled Asian people. In a less organised way there sprung up a number of keep-fit and sewing classes organised by individual women, which obtained small starter grants from the social services community development section.

In comparison to the small amounts of money going out to community organisations in Cleveland, in Manchester, and to some extent in Rochdale, the non-statutory sector received relatively substantial levels of funding under the Inner Areas programme. However, access to Inner Areas funds and its use to develop the non-statutory sector can provide an excuse for not changing mainstream provision. While neighbourhood projects can offer a flexible and accountable service, and theoretically have a demonstration effect on statutory services, the cost for the community is low pay and high levels of voluntary effort. Local authorities are only too often unclear about the remit of community development. Despite the Labour Party's confused ideological position in relation to the non-statutory sector, as a promotion of self-help, in its varying guises, it is on the whole encouraged. To the extent that it increases demands on resources, it may be viewed as a source of irritation.

In Manchester such statutory provision as has been obtained during the period in some ways has been viewed by some groups as encouraging, although developments at both a national and a local level make it clear that there are no safeguards or guarantees in any sphere. The response has been to the fundamental religious and cultural demands, argued through the equal opportunities committee, and in the context of a push for a separate Muslim school should demands not be met. By the end of 1987 the principle of Islamic burial was agreed through the recreation and cultural department. Six trained Urdu teachers and 12 Urdu teaching assistants in secondary schools were reaching an estimated 10 to 12 per cent of the 5,000 or so Muslim school children, and a pilot scheme was introducing halal food in schools in north Manchester. In relation to the single sex schooling issue which had so exercised the Cheetham Muslim community, by the end of 1987, the provision of accompanied coach transport for an ever-increasing number of Muslim girls to Whalley Range school in south Manchester had become an established and popular solution with the parents, although one that was costly to the town hall.

If for the Al-Hilal worker there have been appreciable changes, they have not necessarily been in areas acknowledged as most significant to workers with alternative perspectives, those more concerned with housing allocation, racism in schools, with health issues or the need for counselling provision for young girls and women. The view from each side is that the other represents the interests of the numerical few.

Whatever the difference in perceived priorities within communities, there is also an important gap between the perceptions of community development workers and those of council decision-makers. In a no-growth economy, the reality is that resources can be increased to one group only through a process of redistribution. The community worker on the ground is placed in a position of making difficult choices about where effort is put. The reference has been to unequal levels of status and power, and there is increasing recognition that lack of resources hits black communities far harder than it does the white population. Council politicians and officers, with an eye to political realities, are less ready to make similar choices, even where there is an open recognition of inequalities.

The theory

Our study set out to look at how the worker operated in his or her interaction with the Asian community. Such a relationship was always more than one of individual to community. The factors to be taken into account and the conceptual framework in which that interaction is described must include the community development agency itself and its process of resistance and change, the operation of local politics and community management, and the central importance of racism within the whole.

Writings on community development with Asian groups have tended to isolate parts of what are a complex set of interrelating spheres of action. Much of the attention has been turned towards the community, the model of 'ethnic organisation' having as its twin focus *ethnic unity* and *traditional leadership*. Of the first, Duncan Scott *et al.* write that, 'What we can say is that the sociological evidence convinces us that we are dealing with systems of relationships which are not primarily territorial – the emphasis is on the social network, which may cut across a city, connect with other urban areas and stretch across the world.' (1981, p.32) Indeed we see the Manchester Muslim Parents' Association having reference to similar campaigns in Bradford and Birmingham, while in Rochdale the Bangladeshi community brought in the Bangladesh High Commissioner to settle one inter-factional dispute.

However, what has been more significant has been the inter-play of unity and disunity, a dynamic which has sometimes originated and been promoted by forces *external* to the com-munity. In Manchester the Muslim community, Indians, Pakistanis, Bangladeshis and Malaysians were mobilised in support of the single sex education campaign. Yet it was the perceived challenge by younger black activists to that very influence of the mosque on social and economic life which was manipulated by local politicans and which was to be the critical political factor affecting the outcome of that campaign.

The second focus of the ethnic organisation model has been internal structures and the socio-economic status within Asian communities. This needs to be examined critically. Duncan Scott (1981, p.24) talks of the need 'to identify that entrepreneurial fabric which is so commonly present' and puts forward a 'fundamental lesson' for community workers: 'Locate your con-stituency in a socio-economic sense and then clarify the stage of development of the particular minorities. We need to learn about the *dynamics* of ethnic minorities and if we are to intervene successfully we must be able to locate and mobilise sources of power.'

Given its central objective of widening the base of decision making, the question of community 'leadership' seemed a vital one to RCP when first looking at its own experiences. The issue appeared to be the danger of using direct confrontation in an attempt to introduce more democracy. An early RCP document commented:

The leadership of Asian groups cannot however be equated with that of white groups as in Asian society social groups fulfil a difficult and perhaps more significant function than their white counterparts. They are more powerful and have more responsibility . . . Generally Asian leaders are determined to preserve their own power and the traditional autocratic patterns of community organisation. While such leaders might be very active, it cannot be assumed that these actions are significantly ben-efitting the community.

There is no doubt that such concerns were of importance, and their recognition affected the community development process. In many cases RCP had been able to assist new organisational structures to operate alongside the old sources of patronage and control, in some cases in such a way as to undermine or weaken them. What had been more important in many ways in terms of the outcomes was the external relationships of the community to party political institutions and other intermediaries of the local state. The internal dynamics of the community then acquire their proper significance as they relate to and are acted on by the political environment. The analytical framework needs to be explicitly expanded to include those aspects of the local state and political life as they touch the lives of black people and the workers themselves. Indeed, even our ability to describe events are circumscribed by political sensitivities.

Nationally, the early 1980s had seen council officers and members turning away from the established black community representatives and leaders, and towards other forms of consultation, apparently recognising the diversity of black communities, even their fragmentation, through the funding of smaller voluntary organisations and groups. Ironically, as in the single sex education issue, the acknowledgement of that diversity could also be used to deny the legitimacy of certain claims, or as a reason for withholding the management of resources, or the resources themselves. Furthermore, we have seen how a struggle for resources has frequently served to reinforce division at the expense of a timely political unity. Duncan Scott *et al.* touch on, but fail to develop, the implications.

We are less persuaded of the pluralism because we identify the political and ideological use of ethnicity with a particular societal model, i.e. *one in which the state is not neutral* [my emphasis] and therefore has an interest in particular forms of 'community relations'.

There are different institutional structures which reflect but also distort inter- and intra-group relationships. The model of the worker in the community must then be taken to include the relationship of the community to the institutions of power. The promise of resources to voluntary groups draw those groups into the political process while diverting attention from the real need to change institutions and service provision. In the Milkstone area of Rochdale, the nature of the community's distrust of the local council was a motivating factor for community development; the CBAA area officers had been unable to operate a strategy for community development until that distrust had been eased. In Cleveland it was an understanding of the breakdown of the service infrastructure within the black community which provided a point of departure.

Part of, indeed central to the process then, will be for both black and white groups to recognise racism in society and to direct energy into the struggle against its manifestations at all levels. There are, however, real difficulties for agencies when working against sex and race inequalities when their own structures may contradict and operate against achieving such objectives. This is particularly acute for white-managed agencies when as one worker expressed it, they are 'acting in an oppressive way trying to change oppressive practices within another community'. White workers can find that, identifying themselves as part of something which they are trying to change, there are contraditions which appear to limit action.

Indeed, the power relationship between black and white communities is not just another factor to be considered, but it dramatically affects community development practice and illuminates its analysis. Contributors to this study, motivated to record their own learning experiences of work with black communities, are aware of an inherent difficulty as employees of white-managed or funded agencies. But if their experience is itself a limited one, and restricts the acceptability of the analysis, the perceptions gained through that experience are nevertheless important to grasp.

Principles and practice

The community development initiatives described in this study have had as their prime focus the 'vertical relationship' of communities to power and decision making. The main protagonists have been agencies with differing agendas and priorities; the local authority, the locally-based voluntary group and the intermediary agency, the nature of each reflected in its contrasting approach and style. Each experience, whether within the framework of social action or that of social planning, has thrown up questions about the practice of community development.

A fundamental question for the participants was whether the process of community development with black communities was or should be a different one from that with white communities. Was there anything within the Asian experience which necessitated reassessing the core of principles and practice of community development? Was there indeed such a core, or was it rather that each worker carried to a project a 'baggage of experience' which influenced practice?

Even given the variety of ideological perspectives brought to this study by agencies and individuals, it was nevertheless possible to agree the basics of a list regarding methods and objectives of community development. Although the interpretation and weight given to the various elements was not so clear-cut, there were obvious principles: being non-directive, sharing decision-making and organisational skills, consensus and shared tasks within groups, and encouraging people to take control over their own lives. These were principles which have been generally accepted, especially by employers and funders of community workers (see appendix).

Directiveness of approach had been a major issue for debate between workers, black workers appearing to take, and often justifying a more directive approach, whether because their groups were less familiar with institutional processes, or simply because 'You can't always wait for a community to see the gravity of the situation.' Yet in practice, the principles listed are not always possible or practical even within all-white groups. Those contributing to this study would say that their work with Asian groups indicates that some of the principles or objectives can be even more difficult to achieve in such a context, and that, at the start of that work at least, the worker must be prepared to work with individuals, possibly accept dominant group leaders, even to take on a leadership role if found necessary to establish a working relationship. This then raises the problem of how the worker changes such an emphasis and helps the group to develop a more democratic process of work and decision making. All this takes place in a situation where consensus within a group, between groups, and between groups and the local council can be difficult if not impossible to achieve. Retrospectively, whatever importance was placed on the democratising process, it could be seen that an insistence on purity of method and skills did not relate to anyone's experience of community development. RCP itself could justify its own lack of community accountability in its management structures. In all communities apparently democratic processes, such as election, often mask the holding of power by those familiar with the structures. There is a need to contradict these patterns and work within the community to release confidence, but this is seldom a direct process. In many Asian communities leadership patterns are more structured and more in evidence, apparently demanding an indirect approach, but the results, the change in power holding can be dramatic and quite rapid, as in the case of the Rochdale KYP and Bangladesh projects.

Another objective of community work concerns changing

relationships to power and resources. The principle is that grass-roots work feeds back into institutional change; the practice is that change is focused on the community. Indeed, the job descriptions and community work remit of all the workers in this study only serve to emphasise that point.

Yet if local authorities in particular are serious about responsiveness, they must ensure that change and learning are a two-way process. Work with black communities does not alter this principle, it re-emphasises it. This is pointed up by the qualitative difference between assisting white groups to adapt and work with institutional norms, and doing the same with black groups, when they are excluded from the same institutions. There is an imposition of values and norms external to both black and white communities, but with white communities there is a strong cultural link which does not exist within the older generation in Asian communities. The Al-Hilal worker comments that he had to 'sit down and learn how meetings worked, apologies, minute-taking, etc. Now it is like a piece of cake, but then it was like taking a PhD, everything was so odd and different.' He believed that part of his task was to take community members through the same process of adapting to white institutions, without losing sight of their Muslim identity.

There are central contradictions of agencies working in a class-ridden racist society. Community development has an ideological stand which communities are forced to embrace in order to obtain resources. The dilemma was expressed within the study group in the following way:

We seem to be saying, 'However you used to operate, to succeed you have got to learn to power share, to sit around in groups, and then if you do all that you can have some resources.' But presumably we do believe that there is something inherently worthwhile in people organising in this way, so that people are not so pulled by leadership and can take their own decisions.

Discussion of these principles served to emphasise the importance attached to the *process* in community development rather than the product or goal. But here we entered directly into what had been the most contentious area, in at least the Rochdale team. The issue as it had been debated was whether by entering into casework the workers were guided by a long-term strategy, building confidence and able to tackle other issues. This would bring casework out of the category of service delivery and into the process itself.

However, the question must be taken further, because community development concerns acquiring resources and improving the quality of life for individuals. What the Cleveland workers had found was that black communities were starting from so far back that it was impossible to lay down the casework role, even if this meant they were service providers. Grass-roots work remained important, but primarily as it fed into social planning work. It was a difficult balance, given the need to make up for deficiencies in social services provision. However, there is obviously a point at which the levels of engagement in casework and agency liaison in Cleveland become dysfunctional and the question needs to be posed not as to whether such work is necessary, but does it allow community work to be carried on.

Given the immediacy of the goals which relate to racism, there is a similar dilemma concerning the relationship between community work and direct action. In the case of single sex education in Manchester, it was seen that the achievement of the objective of changed policy appeared to override any objectives in relation to the process of group action. There may be a direct action component to community development, but there are boundaries which are perceived to have been crossed between community worker and community activist. There are obvious risks in this that skills continue to be held by the community worker. Further, we have seen that either failure to achieve the objective, or a perceived loss of 'neutrality' in the eyes of both community or institutions of power, can jeopardise future effectiveness. On the other hand, strategically, short-term successes may give the community the confidence and the political strength to move forward. As one worker expressed it, 'The basics must come first; community development comes later.' In the presence of racism and massive inequalities in the inner city the moral imperatives of going directly for the goal may be overwhelming. Within our group there has been a divergence of views, inconsistency and ambivalence in both its practice and analysis. But there is agreement that community development must adopt a flexible strategy and approach which accommodates the varied economic, political and social realities of the day – the living culture of urban communities.

Postscript

Since completing this study, the questions raised in this chapter have been highlighted further. In a press statement of 3 February 1988, the National Federation of Self-Help Organisations stressed the collapse of some black organisations and the closure of black projects as a result of under-funding: 'Black self-help and community groups in the United Kingdom are now being subjected to the funding-to-fail syndrome by funders, central government, local authorities and others.'

Certainly within the areas we have been looking at there is little confidence that the community initiatives described here can be repeated or indeed sustained. Of major importance is the threat of, or imposition of rate-capping. Manchester City Council faced drastic reductions in its government grant over five years; rate-capping in 1988 forced a decision to cut almost 4,000 jobs and £110 million targetted cut in overall expenditure in the financial year 1988/89. Inevitably uncertainty has hung over projects such as the Al-Hilal project. A second important element has been the growing unreliability of MSC funding as a viable way of resourcing community projects; it had boosted project activity through Community Programme staffing although its limitations had always been clear. Already in the last twelve months there were greater restrictions on the use of such funds and an increased emphasis on training and employment. From September 1988 this emphasis will be reinforced; when the Training Commission replaces the MSC, funds will no longer be used for 'community benefit'. In Rochdale both the Kashmir Youth Project and the Bangladeshi Community Project were extended for a further four years under Inner Areas funding. Sparth Community Centre management committee also secured funding for an additional full-time and two part-time workers from Inner Areas funding. It has not been resolved as to how these projects will be financed when the Inner Areas funds run out.

In Cleveland, many of the agencies which have provided advice services to minority groups have been dependent on Community Programme workers. Yet any assumptions that some of the advice functions may have to be taken on yet further by community workers must contend with the doubts that are being raised about the future direction for community workers themselves, at least for those employed within local authority departments. For Manchester City Council, as employers, it would appear to make increasingly little sense to continue to employ people whose very brief had been to generate a demand for resources within the community, when there was now little possibility of any satisfactory response to those demands.

In Manchester, local politicans have joined council officers in expressing such doubts. For the Labour Party, which retained control of Manchester City Council in the May 1988 elections, there were questions concerning the priority which could be given to community work and the funding of non-statutory organisations against other mainstream, often statutory services. The discussion was not a new one, but there were additional facets to the argument. The concern expressed by community groups themselves as to their future carried less political weight than might have been the case in a pre-election situation. Indeed, there was little political wisdom in supporting community work which aimed at encouraging black and other oppressed and disadvantaged groups to make demands if the city council was increasingly unable to respond positively to such demands without major changes in priorities.

Decentralisation and community consultation had been a major platform for the Labour Party. In a context of financial stringency, such a policy was undoubtedly a resource burden and arguably could be seen to be insubstantial without a lively and well-resourced and structured community basis, but reneging on that policy could not be seen as a likely option.

Against this background it is hardly surprising that community workers themselves were becoming increasingly cynical about their role. The suggestions being made were that a future direction lay either in a closer relationship with social services and community care programmes or with public information and liaison around council initiatives.

Turning to Cleveland and Rochdale, there are pointers indicating that the social planning role of community development workers may be tested as the local authorities themselves extend the language of community development into council services generally. The important question is whether they are able to carry with them to any effect the lessons learnt from the grass-roots experience; this had always been the validation for engagement in social planning. In Cleveland, the second phase of the implementation of decentralisation within the social services department was completed in January 1988. For neighbourhood workers this meant a new management structure and responsibility to the district manager, community and health. Even social services experienced more than usual financial pressure as resources were channelled towards the childcare field following the emergence of the child abuse crisis in 1987.

The county council launched a corporate approach to the needs of unemployed people through the development of an unemployment strategy, a policy with strong political support, involving the bringing together of teams of workers in initially four areas throughout the county, working on a 'community development' model. Extra resources are to be channelled to specific communities suffering multiple deprivation and there will be more direct access to decision-making processes in the county council.

Although one of the areas chosen is a multi-racial area with a strong Asian presence, there is uncertainty as to how far the strategy will address issues of concern to black people. Whilst the neighbourhood work section would wish to influence this process, the unemployment strategy is based within the chief executive's department; the degree of influence it is possible to exert may be limited. Indeed, there are increasing numbers of economic and employment initiatives within both the statutory and voluntary sector, many of which have a specific remit to work with 'minority' groups, and many of which are temporary in nature. Often such schemes claim to be guided by community development principles, but tend to take a fairly directive approach and to be less aware of social and cultural needs.

Within the community development section, on the other hand, a more structured approach to work is being adopted. One result of this is an increasing emphasis on evaluation, which it is hoped will lead to an improvement in the design and execution of projects. Work continues with Asian communities in central Middlesbrough, North Thornaby and South Bank. Thornaby is one of the areas selected under the employment strategy as a community action area and it is, as yet, unclear how the community action workers and the neighbourhood worker will share responsibility for work.

Developments in Rochdale have strong parallels. The Labour Party returned to power in May 1986, taking over from a Liberal/Conservative/SDP alliance. The Labour Party manifesto had laid great emphasis upon establishing a close relationship with the public through a community development approach aligned to a radical reshaping of council structure and organisation and discussions on service delivery.

The first step was to create a community development sub-committee which would develop a consultation report setting out proposals for a decentralisation structure 'enabling local neighbourhood service delivery'. Proposals for the organisation and development of community development services as the basis for overall council service provision would also be developed. In addition, the sub-committee would be responsible for consultations with voluntary organisations and community groups, in particular with regard to the details and mechanisms for decentralised service provision. A restructuring of council departments led to a strengthening of the chief executive's department, hitherto a very traditional council department. The new chief executive and town clerk's department includes a community development division, headed by an assistant chief executive.

The community development division is initiating action in four pilot areas while the council's decentralisation plans are to be refined. Other tasks include the extraction of lessons from Rochdale's experience of previous community-based programmes such as CBAAs and an attempt to bring some coherence to a community development strategy across the borough. Related initiatives are the development of a community recreation service and community education service to draw together various existing initiatives in the pursuit of a coherent community education strategy.

Yet, as in Manchester and Cleveland, the concerns remain. These developments within the local authority have not been matched by resources flowing into the voluntary sector. Community groups with a social emphasis are facing an almost impossible task to secure funding from the Inner Areas Programme which is increasingly earmarked for economic and environmental purposes.

Rochdale Community Project continues to work on issues related to housing and environment improvement within private housing in the context of a Community-Based Action Area Programme which has continued to roll, albeit at a restricted pace. There has been a government redirection of resources away from public improvement of private houses, and RCP is moving generally in the direction of working with the public sector. The CBAA programme itself has completed its work in many of the central areas of Rochdale and has been moved from the planning and estates department to an enlarged housing services department, one which has other functions and may not have the powers of the planning and estates department.

The council has approved a proposal by CPF that it undertakes research and evaluation into the functioning of area committees. An increasing amount of CPF's work relates to liaising and working with organisations such as the evaluation and resource unit within the Greater Manchester area, and with Community Projects Foundation itself in its northern regional strategy.

This development within CPF is symptomatic. Many organisations are moving away from field work and into resourcing; research, evaluation and training is income generating. In a situation where there is a proliferation of agencies competing for a share of a diminishing pool of resources, community development is being forced to be more competitive. If this means defining objectives more clearly, it also means a more concrete style and a value-for-money approach which runs directly counter to the community development ethos of the 1960s and 1970s.

A central contradiction is that increasing numbers of agencies have community dimensions to their work but not the skills nor the time to engage in the essential ground work of community development. In a climate of financial cuts, field work has become a non-essential service. We can see little prospect of viable contact with black communities unless this point is grasped and it remains to be seen whether lessons will be derived from community development experience to point up the essential link between field work and the delivery of services to 'the community', and the complexity of engaging in such work. While we may not have all the answers, we trust that at least some of the questions have been raised in this book.

Appendix: Definition of Community Work

Armstrong *et al* brought together a range of then commonly accepted principles, defining the community work process as:

> . . .carried out with the assistance of an agent of change who, in response to the felt needs of a community will endeavour, using a non-directive technique, to encourage that community to develop its innate potential of self-help, with the participation of as many people as possible, thereby fostering indigenous leadership, in order to achieve certain (process and task) objectives which have been, in consensus, identified by the community as being of benefit to the whole community, and where necessary drawing upon resources external to the community in order to bring to bear an holistic approach to a planned process of change which will be carried out, wherever possible, using a collaborative strategy of action. (1974, p.20)

The Association of Community Workers (ACW) definition of community work, reproduced below, was published in June 1982, and should be seen as a complete statement:

Beliefs

1 The organisation and structure of society cause problems of powerlessness, alienation and inequality. To achieve greater equality and social justice, resources and power must be redistributed.
2 Collective action is a proper and effective method of working for social, political and economic change. Community work is a process which promotes such collective action.
3 It is necessary to confront racism, sexism and other forms of discrimination both within ourselves and within society.

Aims and Objectives

To change power structures by –
- promoting equality of resources
- seeking to influence statutory, voluntary and private organisations and make them more responsive to, and open to the needs and demands of community groups
- assisting groups with multiple disadvantages (for example black groups) to gain access to equal opportunities

To spread knowledge by –
- developing awareness and understanding of issues through social and political education
- enabling people to develop the expertise and skills necessary to further their own objectives
- facilitating access to information

To encourage self-determination by –
- helping community groups to define their own objectives
- supporting community groups to run mutual aid projects

To promote co-operation by –
- the developing of community groups to work on issues of common concern
- seeking to create unity between groups within a locality around issues of common concern, on a basis of mutual respect
- encouraging the development of alliances in order to achieve common goals and influence decision-makers within society

Working Practice

Community workers should work in ways which –
- honestly confront issues of belief and ideology
- start at the point where people themselves identify issues and problems and help them create change in the context of the beliefs above
- always assist people to develop their own leadership and ability to speak for themselves
- respects the contribution made by all people with whom they work, and opposes power relationships

Community workers should not –
- attempt to impose either their own or their employing agencies' concealed ideologies or methods of work

- seek to become spokespersons or leaders of the community or community groups, but they do have the same right and duty as anyone else to accept these roles in situations where that appears to be necessary and appropriate

Notes

1   Agencies and communities

[1] *Report of the Committee on Local Authority and Allied Personal Social Services* (HMSO, 1968).
[2] Gulbenkian Study Group, *Community Work and Social Change* (Longman, 1968).
[3] Gulbenkian Study Group, *Current Issues in Community Work* (Routledge and Kegan Paul, 1973).
[4] J. Harris and E. Crookston, *Asian Survey: Summary Report,* (Cleveland County Research and Intelligence, 1982).
[5] *Report of the Employment/Service Delivery Ethnic Minorities Working Party* (County of Cleveland Social Services, Sept. 1985).
[6] *A Review of Needs, Problems and Trends in Rochdale Borough* (Rochdale Borough Planning and Estates Department, July 1985).
[7] Under Section 11 of the 1966 Local Government Act, local authorities may reclaim from the Home Office 75 per cent of salary costs incurred as the result of making 'special provision' for the needs of commonwealth immigrants 'whose languages or customs differ from those of the community'.
[8] *Poverty in Manchester* (Manchester City Council, Oct. 1986).
[9] *Ethnic Minority Groups in Manchester* (Manchester City Planning Department, Jan. 1984).

2   The framework for action

For much of my description of activities in Sparthbottoms I have drawn freely from a CPF published document, *Design for Living: The Making of a Multi-Cultural Community Centre,* by Mohammed Habeebullah and John Hargreaves with Robert Jeffcoate (1986).

3   Participation or power: the RCP model

[1] Kashmir Youth Project, *Project Criteria*.

4   Roles and rules: access to the community

The case study used here is extracted and condensed from a published article by Ensor, C., *et al*, 'Organising in a multi-ethnic society', in *Community Development Journal*, (April 1982).

5   Towards a team perspective: the worker within the agency

[1]Section 11 of the Local Government Act 1966 entitled certain local authorities 'who are required to make special provision in the exercise of their functions in consequence of the presence within their areas of substantial numbers of immigrants from the Commonwealth whose language or customs differ from those of the community, [to] grants of such amounts as he may with the consent of the Treasury determine on account of expenditure of such descriptions (being expenditure in respect of the employment of staff), as he may so determine' (section 11, Local Government Act 1966). New guidelines introduced in 1982 abolished the rule whereby only local authorities with immigrant populations which had arrived within the previous 10 years could apply; at the same time all new post-holders funded under section 11 were asked to be identified individually.

7   The political content: parties and power struggles

[1] J. Harris, *Consultation with Disadvantaged Groups* (Cleveland County Research and Intelligence Department, April 1985).

8   Organisational Change and Inter-Agency Work

[1] County of Cleveland Social Services, *Report of the Employment/Service Delivery Ethnic Minorities Working Party* (September 1985).

Bibliography

Armstrong, R., and Davies, C. T. *Case Studies in Community Work Vol 1*, University of Manchester, 1974.

Barr, A. 'Community development and minorities: problems and feasible strategies', *Community Development Journal*, October 1980.

Ben-Tovim, G., *et al. The Local Politics of Race*, Macmillan, 1986.

Benn C. and Fairley, J. (eds). *Challenging the MSC on Jobs, Education and Training*, Pluto Press, 1986.

Benyon, J. (ed). *Scarman and After*, Pergamon Press, 1984.

Bishop, J. *Voluntary Sector Local Authority Collaboration on Environmental Improvement*, School for Advanced Urban Studies, Working Paper No. 28, 1983.

Blagg, H., and Dericourt, N. 'Why we need to construct a theory of the state for community work' in Craig, G., Derricourt, N., and Loney, M. (eds). *Community Work and the State*, London: Routledge and Kegan Paul: Association of Community Workers, 1982.

Brown, C. *Black and White Britain: The Third PSI Survey*, London: PSI, 1984.

Boddy, M. and Fudge, C. (eds). *Local Socialism*, Macmillan, 1984.

Bourne, J. 'Towards an anti-racist feminism'. in *Race and Class*, Vol XXC, No 1, Summer 1983.

Cheetham, J. *Social Work and Ethnicity*, London: Allen and Unwin, 1982.

Cheetham, J., *et al. Social and Community Work in a Multi-Racial Society*, London: Harper & Row, 1981.

Community Projects Foundation, *Annual Report 1984–85*.

Connelly, N. *Social Services Departments and Race: A Discussion Paper*, London: PSI Discussion Paper No 2, 1985.

Craig, G., Derricourt, N., and Loney, M. (eds). *Community Work and the State*, London: Routledge & Kegan Paul: ACW, 1982.

Community Relations Commission. *Housing and Ethnic Choice: An Attitude Study*, London, 1977.

Commission for Racial Equality. *Five Views of Multi-Racial Britain*, London, 1978.

Commission for Racial Equality. *Multi-Racial Britain: The Social Services Response*, 1978.

Dungate, M. *A Multi-Racial Society: The Role of National Organisations*, London: Bedford Square Press, 1984.

Ellis, J. 'Management committees and race equality', *Management Development Unit Bulletin (NCVO)*, no 5, June 1985.

Ensor, C., Lambat, I. A., & Scott, D. W. 'Organising in a multi-ethnic society', *Community Development Journal*, April 1982.

Ferns, P., 'The dangerous delusion', *Community Care*, 8 January 1985.

Fitzgerald, M. *Political Parties and Black People: Participation, Representation and Exploitation*, Runnymede Trust, 1984.

Fitzgerald, M. *Black People and Party Politics in Britain*, London, Runnymede Trust, 1981.

Fryer, P. *Staying Power: The History of Black People in Britain*, London: Pluto Press, 1984.

Habeebullah, M., and Hargreaves, J. with Robert Jeffcoate *Design for Living: The Making of a Multi-Cultural Community Centre*, London: Community Projects Foundation, 1986.

Hambleton, R., and Hoggett, P. (eds). *The Politics of Decentralisation: Theory and Practice of a Radical Local Government Initiative*, School for Advanced Urban Studies, Bristol, Working Paper 46, 1984.

Filkin, E., and Naish, M. 'Whose side are we on? The damage done by neutralism' in Craig, G., Derricourt, N., and Loney, M. (eds). *Community Work and the State*, London: Routledge and Kegan Paul/Association of Community Workers, 1982.

Harrison, P. *Inside the Inner City*, Harmondsworth: Penguin, 1983.

Hatch, S., and Humble, S. (eds). *Towards Neighbourhood Democracy*, Arvac Pamplet No 2, 1980.

Henderson, P., and Thomas, D. N. (1980), *Skills in Neighbourhood Work*, London: Allen & Unwin, 1980.

Henderson, P., and Thomas, D. N. *Readings in Community Work*, London: Allen & Unwin, 1981.

Hogget, P. 'Decentralisation, Labourism and the professionalised welfare state apparatus' in Hambleton, R. and Hogget, P. (eds). *The Politics of Decentralisation: Theory and Practice of a Radical Local Government*, School for Advanced Urban Studies, Bristol, Working Paper 46, 1984.

Lawless, P. *Britain's Inner Cities: Problems and Policies*, London: Harper & Row, 1981.

Liverpool Black Caucus. *The Racial Politics of Militant in Liverpool*, Merseyside Area Profile Group and Runnymede Trust, 1986.

Hirst, P. *Community Work: Models and Settings*, Community Projects Foundation, 1983.

Midgely, J., *et al. Community Participation, Social Development and the State*, London: Methuen & Co, 1986.

Miles, R., and Phizacklea, A. *Racism and Political Action in Britain*, London: Routledge & Kegan Paul, 1979.

Ohri, A., *et al. Community Work and Racism*, London: Routledge & Kegan Paul, 1982.

Ousely, H. 'Local Authority Race Initiatives', in Boddy, M. and Fudge, C., *Local Socialism*, MacMillan, 1984.

Prashar, U., and Nicholas, S. *Routes or Roadblocks? Consulting Minority Communities in London Boroughs*, London: Runnymede Trust, 1986.

Scott, D. W., Lambat, I. A., and Ensor, C. 'Strategies for community work in multi-ethnic areas; a paper distributed to community workers in the Greater Manchester Area, 1981.

Sivandandan, A. *A Different Hunger: Writings on Black Resistance*, Pluto Press, 1982.

Sivandandan, A. 'RAT and the deregulation of black struggle', *Race and Class*, vol. 26, no. 4, 1985.

Stoker, G. and Brindley, T. 'Asian politics and housing renewal', in *Power and Politics*, Vol 13 (no 3), 1985.

Stubbs, P. 'The employment of black social workers: from "ethnic sensitivity" to anti-racism?', in *Critical Social Policy*, No 12, Spring, 1985.

Taylor, M., Kestenbaum, A., and Symons, B. *Principles and Practice of Community Work in a British Town*, London: Community Projects Foundation, 1983.

Thomas, D. N. *White Bolts Black Locks: Participation in the Inner City*, London: Allen and Unwin, 1986.

Wilson, A. *Finding a Voice: Asian Women in Britain*, London: Virago, 1978.

Wiseman, P. 'Community work in a multi-racial area', in M. Dungate *et al. Collective Action*, London: Association of Community Workers, 1979.

Young, K. and Connelly, N. *Policy and Practice in the Multi-Racial City*, London: Policy Studies Institute, 1981.

Index

Also published in the **Community Action** series:

Peter Ashby
Trade Unions and the Community: Working for Jobs

Maurice Broady and Rodney Hedley
*Community Partnerships: Community
Development in Local Authorities*

Joan Davidson
*How Green is Your City? Pioneering
Approaches to Environmental Action*

Charmian Kenner
Whose Needs Count? Community Action for Health

Allan McNaught
Health Action and Ethnic Minorities

Barbara Saunders
*Homeless Young People in Britain:
The Contribution of the Voluntary Sector*

Gillian Wilce
*A Place Like Home: A Radical
Experiment in Health Care*

*Grassroots Initiatives:
A Selection from New Society*

INFORMATION CENTRE

BISHOP STREET
LEICESTER

Leicestershire
Libraries & Information Service